MUHURTHA

(Electional Astrology)

BANGALORE VENKATA RAMAN
Editor : THE ASTROLOGICAL MAGAZINE

UBSPD
UBS Publishers' Distributors Ltd.
New Delhi Bombay Bangalore Madras
Calcutta Patna Kanpur London

UBS Publishers' Distributors Ltd.
5 Ansari Road, New Delhi-110 002
Bombay Bangalore Madras Calcutta Patna Kanpur London

Copyright © Dr. B.V. Raman

Eighth Edition	1993
First Reprint	1994
Second Reprint	1994
Third Reprint	1995
Fourth Reprint	1996

All rights reserved. No part of this publication may be reproduced or transmitted in any form or by any means, electronic or mechanical including photocopying, recording, or any information storage and retrieval system, without permission in writing from the publisher.

Printed at Printline, H-8/5 Malviya nagar,
New Delhi-110 017

CONTENTS

Chapter		Page
	Preface to Eighth Edition	v
	Preface to First Edition	vii
I	The Importance of Muhurtha	1
II	General Hints	7
III	The Birth Star and the Birth Moon	16
IV	Influence of Constellations	22
V	Special Adverse Yogas and their Neutralisation	25
VI	On Certain Special Yogas	33
VII	Pre-Natal Ceremonies	35
VIII	Post-Natal Ceremonies	47
IX	Marriage	53
X	Elections Concerning General Matters	88
XI	Elections Pertaining to Education	95
XII	House Building	99
XIII	Agriculture and Farming	113
XIV	Travel	121
XV	Medical Elections	128
XVI	Public Matters	133
XVII	Miscellaneous Elections	137
XVIII	Summary	141
	Appendix I	152
	Appendix II	162
	Appendix III	163
	Bibliography	164
	Index	165

PREFACE TO EIGHTH EDITION

The seventh edition of Muhurtha went out of print more than a year ago. Due to my preoccupations with other activities, the eighth edition could not be brought out earlier.

The edition now presented herewith has been thoroughly revised and at several places entirely re-written with addition of examples for calculating *Thithi, Yoga,* etc.

Much useful information of practical importance has been included in the chapter on "Marriage". Two "Tables" of immediate importance, *viz.*, Table for judging *yoni kuta* or sex-compatibility and the Table for rating the total number of units of agreement for marriage will be found to be of great value to students and practitioners of astrology.

It is hoped that readers will extend to this edition the same enthusiastic reception that they have always done to my other books.

Bangalore   B.V. RAMAN

PREFACE TO FIRST EDITION

There have been many books in recent years on astrology but most of them deal with predictive astrology proper. Muhurtha or Electional Astrology, whilst no doubt an important adjunct to horoscopy, has got its own distinct place in the general scheme of astrological literature. There is perhaps no human activity in the modern times that does not seek the aid of Muhurtha. The justification of this book is therefore that it tries to show that astrology encourages human effort by asking a man to do the right thing at the right moment.

The aim of the book is to present to the reader in a concise form all the essential principles of Muhurtha, so that he could make use of them in all walks of life. A vast literature is extant in Sanskrit on this subject. I have only endeavoured to present in these pages the essential principles culled out from standard works. Where differences were noticeable between two standard works, I have advanced my own views the justification being my humble experience in this line extending over nearly 35 years during which time I have dealt with hundreds of election charts touching almost all human activities. The reader is at liberty to reject my opinions if he feels they do not merit his acceptance.

The aim of astrology is to dispel the fear of the unknown and to give scope for the free play of effort. And MUHURTHA just supplies this want. This treatise is by no means complete. The subject is vast. Yet I have gathered information from many acknowledged sources which, I am sure, will be found to be of the greatest use to the modern man so that instead of merely passing through the formality of astrological consultation, by entrusting the election of a Muhurtha to quacks and montebanks, he may be enabled to so time his activities as to move in harmony with the laws of nature.

Bangalore
1-7-1954

B. V. RAMAN

menal and potential when non-phenomenal. Time therefore can be said to be the basic working power in astrology. This is especially so in Muhurtha as within the time chosen for a particular purpose all the good vibrations have to be centered such that the energy generated would nullify all other unfavourable factors and ensure success of the enterprise.

What is meant by Muhurtha? How far is it superior to horoscopy? These are important questions which we shall try to answer in this chapter. Horoscopy reads what is indicated by the planetary positions at the time of birth being the resultant of one's previous karma. In other words, it has to do only with what one has brought with him - the sum-total of one's inheritance -- physical, mental and material. Here we do nothing more than read simply a technical letter as if it were written in planetary and other symbols. Muhurtha, on the other hand, is much more important. It gives valuable directions by following which the person will be enabled to remove, neutralise, counteract or overcome the evils indicated by the horoscopic chart. Horoscopy is diagnostic. It merely points out the ills but prescribes no remedies. Muhurtha is prescriptive as well as preventive. It tells how by undertaking ventures at auspicious times one can ward off the evils and ensure success. Suppose break in education is indicated by the position of evil planets in the fourth house from the Ascendant and by the affliction of Jupiter, lord of education and Mercury, lord of intelligence. These planetary conjunctions indicate want of education in a man as a result of his karma in previous states of existence. Muhurtha says that the obstructions to educational progress by the planetary conjunctions indicated at the time of birth can be minimised by fixing an auspicious time for commencing the education. Suppose evil planets in the fifth house indicate loss of children. Then Muhurtha comes to his help first by asking him to marry at a certain auspicious time when ethereal currents released from the planets will be so powerful as to minimise or modify the afflictions to the extent that the birth and survival of at least some children may be ensured. Thus Muhurtha helps one to minimise or modify the evils of our past Karma to a considerable extent. I must warn my readers not to imagine that Muhurtha is the master-key to all wealth and happiness. Muhurtha tells us when to do a certain thing if failure is to be avoided.

We have said above that creative, protective and destructive forces are embedded in the womb of Time. As the Sun and the planets are the signatures of time and as all the forces or energies have their source of origin in the Sun, the movements of planets give us a clue as to when the various kinds of creative and destructive forces which are nothing but radiations set in.

Taking an everyday example : nobody could say that the influence of the Sun during the course of one day will be the same. The Sun in the morning, the Sun in the afternoon, the Sun in the evening and the Sun at midnight cannot and will not be the same in heat or in any of his other agencies—light, magnetism, electricity, etc. A man wants to have a picnic and we ask him to have it either in the morning or in the evening when the Sun is not very hot. This will be asking him to reject the noon as inauspicious for pleasure. Here the physical effects are demonstrable to some extent. Similarly a man wants to have a pleasant function. We advise him to have it at a suitable time when, in spite of the season being rainy, there is no chance of the weather being cloudy or rainy. Will we be wrong in asking him to reject the time when the weather is likely to be disturbed ? The same reasoning should guide us to appreciate the idea behind the selection of auspicious times for our various activities. There is a time to sow and a time to reap. Why not we do the sowing operations during harvest season ? Nature would be against us. This is shown by the Sun's position. During the sowing season, creative forces are in operation. When an important activity is to be undertaken, destructive forces have to be screened off. All the planets move incessantly and release different kinds of forces and the Maharshis have given us clues as to how best we can make use of the grand constructive vibrations operating in nature if our endeavours are to be endowed with success.

Even animals instinctively feel that they should move in harmony with nature. For instance, the palolo worm found in the sea around the Fiji Islands reacts in a very definite way to lunar and solar cycles. This animal lives the greater part of its life in deep coral rocks beneath the sea. Towards November, the hind portion of the body becomes distended with migrate eggs. In the early morning, exactly one week after the full moon in November, the hind portion detaches itself as a special reproductive individual which comes to the surface, discharges its eggs in an explosive manner and then dies. There is therefore some sort of an instinctive appreciation on the part of the worm of the Moon's influences, and that the eggs should be discharged only when the planetary vibrations are harmoniously disposed. When such is the case, a human being is to be much more conscious about forces that make or mar his progress and how by the selection of a proper moment, he could take advantage of the constructive forces operating in nature.

Each moment has got its own potency and as Carl Jung says "whatever is born or done this moment of time has the qualities of this moment of time". Hence the moment of birth or the moment at which we elect to do an important act is not certainly an insignificant epoch. Cosmic radiations pouring at the moment on the earth from outer space and coming from various stars and planets act on our brain cells which take up these cosmic radiations which are transformed into vital electricity. It must be noted that in all undertakings invisible energies are set in motion by our words, deeds, thoughts and of course by our actions. You may call these invisible forces as electric, ethereal or electro-magnetic or cosmic radiations. As man himself is an electrical body discharging different kinds of electrical energies, his success and failure are simply matters of attraction and repulsion between himself and the objects with which he has to deal in his day-to-day activities.

Muhurtha could therefore be defined as that precious moment when the vibrations radiated by man are altered to a specific wavelength capable of entering resonance with the radiations of the same vibratory rate coming from other planets and stars.

CHAPTER II

General Hints

A very important place is assigned in Hindu astrology to the part played by the Moon in the fixing of propitious times. The Moon rules the mind and all our psychological inhibitions and his position in the election chart is to be particularly dignified. Moreover, whenever an election is to be made, it should always bear a sympathetic connection with the birth chart. Should the radical horoscope indicate several afflictions, no Muhurtha can ensure real success. In fact, the strength of the birth chart may even prevent the person from taking advantage of the propitious period. Or at best, the chances of failure may be somewhat minimised. There is, therefore, an important factor to be considered, *viz.*, whether the birth chart is really so powerfully afflicted as to offset the chances of success shown in the election chart. When people do not know the birth chart, the best thing would be to ascertain their name constellation (see Appendix at the end of the book) and study the transit influences operating at the period in question. Whether or not the radical chart is strong, Hindu astrology always takes cognisance of the fact that contact is maintained between the Janma Tara (the constellational position of the Moon at the time of one's birth) and if the birth time is not known, with the Nama-Tara (name-constellation), and the election chart.

Whilst it is necessary to bear in mind that the election chart is likely to be affected by the benefic or malefic nature of the directions operating at the moment in the birth chart and the inherent strength of the horoscope, it is not necessary to go into it in detail. A number of combinations is given in ancient works to so strengthen the election chart as to make it fruitful independent of the birth influences. These details will be discussed in their appropriate places.

Before we take up electional astrology proper, a short description of the Panchanga or the Hindu almanac is very necessary, as the important items constituting a Panchanga have an intimate bearing on the fixing of auspicious times. The Panchanga consists of five limbs or accessories, *viz.*, Tithi (lunar day), Vara (weekday), Nakshatra (constellation), Yoga (a luni-solar day), and Karana (half a lunar day). The reader will have to be familiar with these technicalities though by far the most mportant ones are the lunar day, constellation and weekday. The five limbs of the Panchanga are supposed to represent the five sources of ethereal energy of which some are visible and others invisible and which when properly secured are said to conduce the health, wealth and prosperity of mankind.

Tithi.—This is the time during which the difference of the increment of longitude of the Sun and the Moon amounts to 12°. The lunar day is to the Hindu of the most prominent practical importance, since by it are regulated the performance of many religious ceremonies and upon it depend the chief considerations of Muhurtha or electional astrology. In other words, the tithi represents the lunar energy, and lunar energy is identified with mental energy. Therefore a minute knowledge of the

General Hints

lunar movements constituting tithis is said to give us wealth.

Each tithi (See Table II) or lunar day is equal to 0.9483 of a day so that a lunar month is equal to about 29.53 days. The ending time of a tithi is the moment at which the Moon is removed from the Sun by multiples of 12°. Thus when the Moon is 12° away from the Sun, the first lunar day or Prathama ends; when 24° Dwitiya and so on; when in conjunction the Amavasya (New Moon), and when in opposition (180°) Pournimasya (full Moon) ends.

It is enough for astrological purposes to know what *tithi* rules at the time of birth.

To find the lunar day or tithi deduct the longitude of the Sun from that of the Moon. If the difference is less than 180°, it is the bright half or Sukla Paksha; if it is more than 180°, it is the dark half or Krishna Paksha.

Divide the balance (Moon-Sun) by 12° (or 720'). The quotient represents the number of tithis elapsed and the remainder the part of the next (current) tithi that has elapsed.

Thus to know the tithi ruling on 8-8-1895 at 4^h 10^m 20^s (L.M.T.) at Bangalore. First we deduct the longitude of the Sun (114° 40' or 6880') from that of the Moon (326° or 19560'). The remainder is 211° 20' (12680'). It is more than 180° and hence it is the dark half (Krishna Paksha). Dividing by 12° (or 720') the quotient is 17, which means the lunar day is the 18th (or 3rd lunar day of the dark half). 440' (7° 20') of its portion has been traversed, leaving 280' (4° 40') yet to be traversed. If this remainder is multiplied by 24 and divided by the difference of the daily motions of the Sun and the Moon, we get the number of hours (from the time of birth or question) still covering the tithi in question.

Suppose the daily motion of the Moon on the day of birth is 11° 47'
*Daily motion of the Sun 57'
_____
10° 50'
Difference : = 650'

Multiplying 280 by 24 and dividing the product by 650 we get

$$\frac{280 \times 24}{650} = 10h. \ 57m.$$

which added to the given time gives 3h. 27m. = 3h. a.m. (on 9th August) which will be the ending moment of the tithi (3rd lunar day of the dark half).

Vara.—This is of course the ordinary weekday. The weekdays are named in accordance with certain astronomical considerations. Therefore on a weekday bearing the name of a particular planet, the influence of that planet is said to be predominant.

The weekdays are numbered thus: Sunday 1, Monday 2, Tuesday 3, Wednesday 4, Thursday 5, Friday 6 and Saturday 7.

Nakshatra.—The zodiac is marked by 27 constellations or nakshatras often termed lunar mansions. The position of a nakshatra is dependent upon the actual time taken by the Moon to traverse 13° 20.' of ecliptic arc, of course, always beginning from the first point of the constellational zodiac. If constellations are huge electromagnetic bodies radiating energy into space, there seems to be sense in attributing certain influences to these radiations and the Moon coming into contact

---

* For convenience sake more than 30" are taken as 1' and less than 30" rejected.

General Hints

with such radiations probably exercises special influences. The Janma Tara (birth constellation) or Dina Tara (the constellation of the day concerned) is obtained thus:

The ecliptic is divided into 27 constellations (See Appendix III) of $13° 20'$ (or $800'$ of arc) each. Reduce the longitude of the Moon to minutes and divide the same by 800. The quotient is the number of constellations already passed, and the remainder, the part covered in the current asterism the Moon is in. For the data given under tithi.

The Moon is in Aquarius $\quad 25° 59' 46''$
$= 10$ signs $25° 59' 46''$
$= 325° 59' 46''$
$= 19559' 46''$

Dividing this by 800 $\quad \dfrac{19559' 46''}{800}$

$=$ Quotient 24
remainder $359' 46''$

The ruling star is the 25th, *viz.*, Poorvabhadra. $359' 46''$ have been covered in this star and the balance to be traversed is $(800' - 359' 46'')$.

Yoga.—It is the period during which the joint motion in longitude of the Sun and the Moon amounts to $13° 20'$. Every Hindu almanac contains a column specifying the yoga for each day and when it would end. There are twenty-seven yogas (see Appendix IV).

Yoga represents a conjunction of subtle influences which strengthen our bodies, remove the germs of disease, and help us to enjoy health and life in its various phases.

YOGA

The following formula is according to *Suryasiddhanta* :

$$\frac{\text{Sun's longitude} + \text{Moon's longitude}}{13° 20' \text{ (or } 800')}$$

Taking the example date given under tithi :

Sun's longitude	114°	40'
Moon's longitude	326°	0'
Total	440°	40'
=	80°	40'
=		4840'

Dividing 4840' by 800 we get quotient 6 and remainder 40. 6 Yogas have transpired and the 7th, *viz*, Sukarman is ruling. 40' is the part of the current (Sukarman) that has elapsed. Yet to be covered in this Yoga is 760'. To ascertain the time at which the current Yoga ends, divide 760' by the sum of the daily motions of the Sun and the Moon (0° 57' + 11° 47' = 12° 44' or 764') and multiply by 24 to reduce the results to hours.

$$\frac{760 \times 24}{764} = 23\text{h. }50\text{m.}$$

The Sukarman Yoga ends at 23h. 50m. from the time of birth or any given time.

The Table of Yogas (*Appendix IV*) enables one to ascertain the Yoga on the basis of the joint motion of the Sun and the Moon.

Thus in the example the sum of the Sun's and the Moon's longitude is 80° 40'. According to *Appendix IV* Sukarman commences at 80° and extends till 93° 20'.

Karana.—And finally we have karana, or half a lunar day meaning thereby the time taken to complete the distance which should be the multiple of 6 between the Sun and the Moon. There are 11 karanas, *viz.*, (1) Bava,

General Hints

(2) Balava, (3) Kaulava, (4) Taitula, (5) Garija, (6) Vanija, (7) Visti, (8) Sakuna, (9) Chatushpada, (10) Naga and (11) Kimstughna. The first seven come by rotation eight times in a lunar month, commencing with the second half of the first lunar day. The last four are said to be permanent karanas and occur in order with the second half of the 29th lunar day.

In Muhurtha, it is always advisable to strengthen the ascendant and its lord and the Moon. Each type of election requires fortification of some appropriate house and planet and these will be discussed in their proper places. Even when the ascendant is strong, certain parts of it which go under the name of *Lagna tyajya* should be rejected. Sometimes, only fixed signs are to be chosen; sometimes only movable signs are to be chosen. Hence, a reader has to very carefully understand these subtle distinctions.

In Aries, Taurus, Sagittarius and Virgo, the first three degrees should be avoided as it is supposed to be in the nature of a serpent *(bhujanga)* and hence destructive. In regard to Pisces, Capricorn, Cancer and Scorpio, the last (three degrees) has to be avoided as it is supposed to be presided over by the evil force of Rahu. The middle half ghati ($13° 30'$ to $16° 30'$) should be rejected with regard to Gemini, Libra, Leo and Aquarius as it is ruled by an evil force termed Gridhra.

Tuesday and Saturday should be avoided for all good and auspicious works.

The 4th, 8th, *12th and 14th lunar days both in the bright and the dark halves are unsuitable for undertaking any auspicious work.

---

* In our experience, the 12th lunar day is quite auspicious; provided the other factors are strong, 12th lunar day can be employed for auspicious works.

Each constellation has its own *tyajyakala* or negative period which is to be invariably avoided. The negative periods commence at the times marked below against each constellation lasting for 4 ghatis (1 hour 36 minutes) from thence.

Aswini 50 ; Bharani 4 ; Krittika 30 ; Rohini 40 ; Mrigasira 14 ; Aridra 21 ; Punarvasu 30 ; Pushya 20 ; Aslesha 32 ; Makha 30 ; Pubba 20 ; Uttara 1 ; Hasta 21 ; Chitta 20 ; Swati 14 ; Visakha 14 ; Anuradha 10 ; Jyeshta 14 ; Moola 20 ; Poorvashadha 20 ; Uttarashadha 20 ; Sravana 10 ; Dhanishta 10 ; Satabhisha 18 ; Poorvabhadra 16 ; Uttarabhadra and Revati 30.

In the scheme that is followed, I have first of all dealt with the pre-natal and post-natal ceremonies which are designated as Shodasa Karmas which every Hindu is supposed to undergo in his life's journey from cradle to the grave. Some of these ceremonies such as baptising, first feeding, marriage, etc., are common to all communities so that non-Hindus can make use of them with equal benefit.

The Shodasa Karmas (sixteen kinds of ceremonies), which a Hindu is enjoined to undergo, seem to have been based upon certain critical psychological and physiological developments (climacterics) which occur in a man's life at certain definite intervals. It must be noted that the successive stage when the human infant assumes the upright posture, commences to speak and so on, occur at fixed times in normal development so much so that a child that does not begin to talk or walk at the proper time becomes a source of anxiety to his parents. The change of teeth also marks a transition. Permanent dentition sets in about 7 years after birth. Seven years after this another crisis is reached and that is puberty. A further change is noted about the age of

21. There are of course several other critical periods such as the menopause occurring at the age of 49 or 50 (7 × 7), another grand climacteric at 63 (7 × 9) often accompanied by death. In the human being, it is said that every cell of the body is renewed every seven years, although this is not quite correct for all tissues. Thus, the *Shodasa Karmas* are supposed to fortify the human body and human mind at such critical phases. Perhaps a deeper study of the problem will reveal a more correct perspective of the rationale.

CHAPTER III

The Birth Star and the Birth Moon

In fixing auspicious times, apart from the special planetary combinations to be applied for specific purposes, there are three factors which are common to almost all elections and which require the astrologer's most careful attention. They are (*a*) Tarabala or strength of constellation, (*b*) Chandrabala or lunar strength, and (*c*) Panchaka or five-source energy. These three should be satisfactorily disposed. Otherwise an election chart will lose its significance.

Strength of Constellation.—The constellation ruling at the time of birth is one's Janmanakshatra or birth star and the zodiacal sign in which the Moon is situated at the time of one's birth is one's Janma Rasi or Birth Moon. These are highly important. Count from the birth constellation to the one ruling on the particular day on which a new work is to be done or a journey undertaken and divide the number by 9 if divisible. Otherwise keep it as it is. If the remainder is 1 (janma) it indicates danger to body; if 2 (sampat) wealth and prosperity; if 3 (vipat) dangers, losses and accidents; if 4 (kshema) prosperity; if 5 (pratyak) obstacles; if 6 (sadhana) realisation of ambitions; if 7 (naidhana) dangers; if 8 (mitra) good; and if 9 (parama mitra) very favourable. There are certain exceptions to the favourable and unfavour-

The Birth Star and the Birth Moon

able results ascribed above and they will be dealt with in the appropriate places.

Example :—A man born in Aswini elects to undertake a journey on a day ruled by Sravana. Counting from the man's Janma Nakshatra to the one ruling on the proposed day, the number will be 22. This divided by 9 leaves a remainder of 4. This goes under *kshema* or favourable and hence Tarabala is good.

When the day's nakshatra falls in the first Paryaya or cycle, that is within the first nine stars, the evil suggested above, *viz.*, 3rd star Vipat, 5th star Pratyak, etc., holds good in full.

In the Second Paryaya or cycle, *e.g.*, Janma Nakshatra, etc., falling from the 10th to 18th, the evil is said to be only fiffy per cent. In fact the evil is centred only in the first quarter of the 3rd (Vipat), the 4th quarter of the 5th (Pratyak) and the 3rd quarter of the 7th (Naidhana) of the second cycle.

In the third cycle or *Paryaya*, the Janma, Vipat, etc., falling from the 19th to 27th the evil is said to be almost negligible. Suppose the birth star is Rohini and the day's star is Satabhisha. The day's star counted from birth star comes to 21, or the 3rd in the third cycle. The 3rd is Vipat. But it is said to carry little or no evil.

In my humble experience, it is better to avoid *Vipat* and *Naidhana* stars for all important undertakings—long journeys, marriage, starting of an enterprise, etc., even if such a star happens to fall in the 3rd-cycle, unless there are other counteracting factors.

According to some classical writers, the 22nd and 27th stars are always inauspicious. But our experience is to the contrary. The 22nd is always *sadhana* and the

27th *parama mitra* and hence they could be considered as auspicious.

Chandrabala.—As we have already said above, the consideration of the Moon and his position are of much importance in Muhurtha. To be at its best, the Moon should not occupy in the election chart, a position that happens to represent the 6th, 8th or 12th from the person's Janma Rasi.

To take another example: a person born in Mrigasira (Janma Rasi being Taurus) wants to have his marriage on a day ruled by Bharani which means the Moon will be in Aries. There is neither Tarabala (as Bharani will be Naidhana to Mrigasira) nor Chandrabala (the Moon on the election day falls in Aries which would be the 12th from the subject's Janma Rasi). Hence, the day is most inauspicious. Certain constellations, apart from their being harmonious or otherwise disposed with reference to one's own Janma Nakshatra, should be avoided for certain specific purposes on account of their *inherent* evil natures. In fact, Bharani is condemned for all good work and it has to be scrupulously avoided for all good work.

Panchaka (Five-Source Energy).—For matters of ordinary importance such as interviewing superiors or going on short journeys, a favourable Tarabala will do and there is no need to consider the panchaka. But in regard to very important ceremonies such as marriage, nuptials, entry into new houses, etc., this should be carefully looked into. There are several methods by which panchaka is determined. I shall give the most common method. In the panchaka determination, apparently, five sources of planetary, stellar and zodiacal energies are involved. Take the number of the lunar day (from the 1st of the month), the number of the weekday,

Sunday 1, etc.), the number of the constellation (from Aswini) and the number of the Lagna (from Aries). Add these together and divide the total by 9. If the remainder is 1 (mrityu panchakam), it indicates danger; if 2 (agni panchakam), risk from fire; if 4 (raja panchakam), bad results; if 6 (chora panchakam), evil happenings and if 8 (roga panchakam), disease. If the remainder *is 3, 5, 7 or zerothen it is good*. As an example, let us assume that A wants to start a business on a day and time otherwise conforming to the requirement of Muhurtha—the constellation being Aslesha, the lunar day being the 13th, the rising sign being Virgo and the weekday Sunday. Calculating the panchaka, we get —

Number of the lunar day	13
Number of constellation	9
Number of weekday	1
Number of zodiacal sign	6
	29

Dividing this by 9, we get $29/9 = 3\ 2/9 - 2$ as remainder. It indicates Vahni or fire and hence the time selected is not favourable. In dealing with this subject, Prof. B. Suryanarain Rao observes thus in his famous book ASTROLOGICAL MIRROR : "There are many things as in medicine, so in astrology which when properly understood and followed would tend to minimise the chances of evil influences indicated by planets, lunar days, constellations and rising signs and in all these the idea seems to be to avert the evils which would arise as a matter of fact from the attraction or combination of the subtle influences contained in time and the chemical changes which arise from the conjunctions and repulsions of various forms of energies, some of which are visible, while many of which ars subtle and very mysterious in their nature."

The general rule of avoiding unfavourable panchaka has certain exceptions. When an election is to do with occupation, avoid *Raja Panchaka*. In elections bearing on house building, avoid both *Raja* and *Agni Panchakas*. In regard to travel, *Chora Panchaka* should be rejected. In marriage and upanayanam, *Roga* and *Mrityu Panchakas* should be avoided. Conversely it also means that a panchaka declared unsuitable for a particular type of election could be used for a different kind of election. No astrological authority has specifically approved this step but by implication, we can assume that there is no objection if, for instance, we ignore raja panchaka for travelling or marriage or roga panchaka for house-building. As far as possible, it is advisable to avoid the evil of panchaka in general irrespective of its definite bearing on an election. But when a more auspicious day cannot be secured, we can resort to the lesser of the two evils.

As regards Tarabala referred to above, it is no doubt advisable to avoid a day that is ruled by the 1st, 3rd, 5th and 7th constellations. But when the day is otherwise favourable, only the negative parts of these unfavourable constellations may be avoided. Thus, in the Janma, Vipat, Pratyak and Naidhana constellations, the first 7, 3, 8 and 6 ghatis respectively may be considered evil and avoided. Thus, a man whose Janma Nakshatra is Pushyami can undertake a venture on a day ruled by Makha (Vipat) provided he avoids the first seven ghatis of the constellation. The stigma attached to the star being Vipat no longer holds good. Generally these exceptions are resorted to only under special circumstances when an election is to be urgently made and when the undertaking admits of no delay.

A day ruled by one's Janma Nakshatra is ordinarily held to be unfavourable for an election. But in regard to nuptials, sacrifices, first feeding, agriculture, upanayanam, coronation, buying lands, learning the alphabet, Janma Nakshatra is favourable without exception. But it is inauspicious for war, sexual union, shaving, taking medical treatment, travel and marriage. For a woman, Janma Nakshatra would be quite favourable for marriage.

There are several technicalities to be considered in the selection of auspicious times and in spite of the apparent inconsistencies to be found in the opinions expressed by different classical writers on this subject, I have endeavoured to give the easiest and what, in my humble opinion, are the most reliable principles bearing on this all-important subject.

CHAPTER IV

Influence of Constellations

The whole of Muhurtha or for that matter, the whole of Hindu astrology is based on the movements of planets in relation to the constellations. The wisdom of the ancient Indians in making predictive astrology, dependent upon the fixed zodiac, is being increasingly appreciated by students of the science. The question of zodiacal influences hinges on the fact whether the star-points or constellations with which the Sun comes into line from day-to-day derive their influences from that body or irrespective of the shifting position of the Sun, there is any special virtue attaching to these star-points. We have shown with incontrovertible evidence in several of our articles in THE ASTROLOGICAL MAGAZINE that the stars have a decided influence on all human affairs and we have several times disproved the absurd views displayed by the so-called scientists that because stars are removed millions and billions of miles away from us, there cannot be any connection between those gigantic masses and the living human beings. These electro-magnetic bodies are capable of discharging different kinds of energies manifesting themselves in different ways. When a constellation like Bharani (β Arietis) is held to be constitutionally unfit for certain types of elections ; it means that the vibrations emanating from it are destructive in character.

Influence of Constellations

I do not propose to discuss here the astrological influences of the various constellations elaborately. I would give just the important ones, mainly based on BRIHAT SAMHITA and leave the reader to refer to more standard works on Muhurtha for further details.

The 28 constellations (including Abhijit which is generally ignored in everyday astrological consultations) are presided over by Aswini, Yama, Agni, Prajapati, the Moon, Rudra, Aditi, Jupiter, Serpent, Pitrus or manes, Bhaga, Aryaman, Savita, Swashta, Vayu, Indragni, Mitra, Indra, Niruti, Visvedewa, Brahman, Vishnu, Vasu, Varuna, Ajaikapat, Ahirbudhnya and Pushan respectively.

Rohini, Uttara, Uttarashadha and Uttarabhadra are supposed to be fixed constellations and they are favourable for coronations, laying the foundations of cities, sowing operations, planting trees and other permanent things.

Chitta, Anuradha, Mrigasira and Revati are *soft* constellations. They are good for wearing new apparel, learning dancing, music and fine arts, sexual union and performance of auspicious ceremonies.

Aswini, Pushya, Hasta and Abhijit are *light* constellations, and they can be selected for putting ornamentation, pleasures and sports, administering medicine, starting industries and undertaking travels.

Moola, Jyestha, Aridra and Aslesha are sharp in nature and they are favourable for incantations, invoking spirits, for imprisonment, murders, and separation of friends.

Saravana, Dhanishta, Satabhisha, Punarvasu and Swati are movable stars and they are auspicious for acquiring vehicles, for gardening and for going on procession.

Pubba, Poorvashadha and Poorvabhadra, Bharani and Makha are dreadful stars and they are suitable for nefarious schemes, poisoning, deceit, imprisonment, setting fire and other evil deeds.

Krittika and Visakha are mixed constellations and during their influences, works of day-to-day importance can be undertaken.

Beginning from the third quarter of Dhanishta and ending with the last part of Revati, the time is held to be unsuitable for any kind of auspicious work. This period goes under the special name of Nakshatra Panchaka and when these stars are ruling, one should avoid journey towards the south, house repairing or renovation, collecting fuel and cattle fodder or acquiring cots and beds.

Of all the twenty-eight constellations, the pride of place appears to have been given to Pushya, the 8th star.

The constellation of Pushya is supposed to be the most favourable of all the 28 constellations. It is said to neutralise almost all doshas or flaws arising out of a number of adverse combinations. The Rishis go to the extent of saying that even if unfavourable combinations are present in the birth horoscope hampering one's success in life, and the ruling constellation and the position of the Moon are all adverse, Pushya has the power of neutralising these evil forces and asserting its benefic nature. In spite of all the benefic influences attributed to Pushya, it is held to be inauspicious for purposes of marriage. There may be an element of exaggeration in the assertion that Pushya is capable of modifying all the evil influences present in an election chart but there is no doubt whatsoever that it is a constellation *par excellence* that could be universally employed for all purposes, excepting of course marriage.

CHAPTER V

Special Adverse Yogas and their Neutralisation

The farmers of the astrological rules were not mere theoreticians. They were practical men and did not beleive, in merely cataloguing their observations for academical purposes. Whilst it is always desirable to fix a Muhurtha that is auspicious by all standards of astrological rules, there would sometimes be practical difficulties and emergent occasions which admit of no delay. Therefore, emphasis is laid on what is called *gunabahulya* or excess of good and *dosha swalpa* or deficiency of evil. When one has to visit a friend or a relation, who is seriously ill in a far-off place, we are asked not to attach any consideration to the astrological factors. Because at a moment's notice it is impossible to get a time which could be deemed to be propitious astrologically. But when one is to go on a pilgrimage or a business tour or for a marriage, one should see that he starts under influences that are harmoniously disposed towards him.

There are said to be 21 great evils (*ekavimsati mahadoshas*) which are to be avoided for any auspicious work. But when one finds it difficult to avoid them because of astrological impossibility or circumstantial inability, one can take advantage of the neutralising combinations which are generally supposed to act as antidotes. We may just make a passing reference to these 21 great evils for the information of the readers. They are :—

1. *Panchanga Suddhi.*—We have already said that a Panchanga consists of *tithi, vara, nakshatra, yoga* and *karana*. All these must be auspicious. In regard to lunar days, the 4th, 6th, 8th, 12th and 14th, full and new moon days should be avoided. In regard to *vara,* Thursday and Friday are held to be suitable for all works. Tuesday is to be generally avoided except when it happens to be the 10th, 12th or 16th day of the child's birth when the child's Namakarana (baptising or giving name) may be performed. Of the several Nakshatras, Bharani and Krittika should be avoided for all auspicious works as these two are said to be presided over by the god of death (Yama) and the god of fire (Agni) respectively. In urgent cases if the Lagna could be fortified, the *dosha* due to nakshatra may get neutralised. The last parts of Aslesha, Jyeshta and Revati should also be avoided. Coming to the Yoga (*vide* page 12) the 6th (Atiganda), 9th (Soola), 10th (Ganda), 17th (Vyatipata) and 27th (Vydhruti) have deleterious effects upon events which are started or commenced under them. The Karana chosen must be appropriate to the election in view. Thus *Bava* is auspicious for starting works of permanent importance while *Thaithula* is propitious for marriage. *Bhadra* is unfit for any good work but is eminently suitable for violent and cruel deeds. For getting initiation into kshudra mantras *Sakuni* Karana is propitious.

Therefore, Panchanga Suddhi means a good lunar day, a beneficial weekday, an auspicious constellation, a good yoga and a fertilising Karana.

2. *Surya Sankramana.*—The 2nd great evil is Surya Sankramana or the solar ingress into different zodiacal

signs. When the Sun is about to leave one sign and enter another there seem to occur certain disturbances in the organisation of the solar forces and such times are not recommended for any good work. On the contrary, they are held to be propitious for meditation, initiation into secret mantras and performance of certain religious rites which are held to purify not only the bodily electrical discharges but also the mental currents. Sixteen ghatis (6 hours 24 minutes) both before and after the entry of the Sun into a new sign should be rejected for all new works.

3. *Karthari Dosha*.—Karthari means scissors. In an election, when two evil planets are placed on either side of the Lagna, the combination goes under the special name of Karthari Dosha and it should be rejected for good work particularly in regard to marriage.

4. *Shashtashta Riphagatha Chandra Dosha.—The* Moon should invariably be avoided in the 6th, 8th and 12th houses from the Lagna rising in an election chart.

5. *Sagraha Chandra Dosha*.—The Moon's association with any other planet, benefic or malefic, should be avoided. This injunction is specially applicable in case of marriage.

6. *Udayasta Suddhi.*—The Lagna and the seventh should be strong. The Lagna should be occupied by its own lord and the Navamsa Lagna by its own lord or *vice versa* or lord of Lagna should aspect Navamsa Lagna and *vice versa*. Similarly the seventh and the lord of the seventh Bhava should be favourably disposed. The strength of Lagna and the seventh is necessary in all elections but especially so in regard to marriage.

7. *Durmuhurtha*.—Muhurtha technically means 48 minutes or 2 ghatis in terms of time. A sidereal day

consists of 30 muhurthas. The 1st fifteen diurnal muhurthas named are: (1) Rudra, (2) Ahi, (3) Mitra, (4) Pitru, (5) Vasu, (6) Vara, (7) Vishwedeva, (8) Vidhi, (9) Sathamukhi, (10) Puruhuta, (11) Vahini, (12) Naktanchara, (13) Varuna, (14) Aryama and (15) Bhaga. The nocturnal muhurthas are: (1) Girisa, (2) Ajipada, (3) Ahirbudhnya, (4) Pusha, (5) Aswi, (6) Yama, (7) Agni, (8) Vidhatru, (9) Chanda, (10) Aditi, (11) Jeeva, (12) Vishnu, (13) Yumigadyuti, (14) Thyasthur and (15) Samdram.

In regard to the diurnal muhurtha, the 1st, 2nd, 4th, 10th, 11th, 12th and 15th are inauspicious while in nocturnal muhurthas the 1st, 2nd, 6th and 7th are inauspicious.

In calculating the muhurtha, the exact length of day and night should be ascertained. Each muhurtha is said to last for 48 minutes (2 ghatis) on the assumption that the duration of day and night is of equal proportion, *viz.*, 30 ghatis, or 12 hours. If the length of day is 28 ghatis, then each muhurtha extends for 1 ghati and 52 vighatis ($20^h\ 20^s.\ 8$).

Apart from the above general classification of good and bad muhurthas, the following should also be deemed as unpropitious on the different weekdays. Sunday coinciding with the 14th lunar day (Aryama) ; Monday the 8th (Vidhi) and the 12th (Naktanchara) ; Tuesday the 4th (Pitru) and the 11th (Vahni) ; Wednesday (Abhijit) ; Thursday the 12th (Naktanchara) and 13th (Varuna) ; Friday the 4th (Pitru) and the 8th (Vidhi) and Saturday the 1st (Rudra) and the 2nd (Ahi).

Particularly in marriages, the muhurthas declared above as inauspicious in regard to **weekdays should not** be considered.

8. *Gandanthara.*—The last 2 ghatis (48 minutes) of the 5th, 10th and 15th (Full Moon) and the first 2 ghatis of the 6th, 11th and 1st (dark half) lunar days go under *tithigandanthara* and they should be rejected for all new works. Similarly, the last 2 degrees of Cancer, Scorpio and Pisces and the first 2 degrees of Leo, Sagittarius and Aries are inauspicious. The last ghatis of Aslesha, Jyeshta, Moola, Revati and Aswini and the first four ghatis of Makha should be avoided as injurious for good work.

Papashadvarga.—Malefics should not be strong in shadvargas in an election chart.

10. *Bhrigu Shatka.*—The position of Venus in the 6th is injurious. This is especially so in regard to marriage. Even when Venus is exalted and associated with benefics, such a disposition is not approved.

11. *Kujasthama.*—Mars should be avoided in the 8th house, as it indicates destruction of the object in view. In a marriage election chart, Mars in the 8th is unthinkable. Even if Mars is otherwise powerful, he should not occupy the 8th house.

12. *Ashtama Lagna Dosha.*— In selecting a time for marriage, the Lagna ascending should not happen to be the 8th from the Janma Lagna of the bride and the bridegroom. Suppose the would-be husband and wife are born in Aquarius and Capricorn respectively. At the time of marriage, the ascending Lagna should be a sign other than Virgo or Leo as these two happen to be the 8th from the bridegroom and bride's Janma Lagnas respectively.

13. *Rasi Visha Ghatika.*— Elsewhere has been given the negative periods of different Lagnas (Lagna Thyajya). They are to be rejected for all auspicious work.

14. *Kunavamsa Dosha.*—The Lagna selected for an auspicious work should not occupy the Navamsa of a malefic.

15. *Varadosha.*—This has already been explained on page 26. Certain weekdays are to be avoided for certain special activities.

16. *Grahanothpatha Dosha.*—The constellations in which the eclipses appear should be avoided, and in regard to marriage, such a constellation should be avoided for six months.

17. *Ekargala Dosha.*—This dosha is powerful only during the daytime. Affects matters started under certain yogas such as Vishkhambam. We need not go into details as it is not of much significance.

18. *Krura Samyuta Dosha.*—The constellation occupied by the Sun at a given moment, and the one immediately preceding and succeeding it have to be deemed unpropitious for all good work and they should be rejected for purposes of marriage.

19. *Akalagharjitha Vrishti Dosha.*—When there is rainfall and thunder, out of season, such days should be deemed unfit for all good work.

20. *Mahapatha Dosha.*—When the Sun and the Moon are equally removed from the equator upon the same side of it, the aspect is known as Vyatipata, which indicates excess of evil. This is held to be unfavourable for all good work.

21. *Vaidhruthi Dosha.*—This is also an evil aspect (yoga) and should be avoided in all favourable activities.

I have given above a fairly clear description of the 'evils', which are generally to be met with in all classical works on Muhurtha. The reader should not get scared away at the thought of these large number of doshas or planetary evils which are to be avoided if one is to elect

Special Adverse Yogas and their Neutralisation

a proper time for the fruition of an object in view. Man has to contend against a stupendous number of evil agencies or discordant vibrations released by the planetary bodies and each of these *mahadoshas* seems to express euphemestically the particular types of evil energies which would affect adversely particular types of human activities. There are several exceptions to these general doshas. One should always remember that in electing a suitable moment one should try to avoid the major doshas by fortifying the ascendant and taking advantage of the exceptions and ignoring the minor ones.

The following combinations are held to neutralise the adverse yogas mentioned above:

1. The *lagnathyajya* referred to *supra* prevails only on particular days as per details below. In the first Navamsa—Wednesday and Saturday. In the middle Navamsa—Monday and Friday. In the last Navamsa—Tuesday, Thursday and Sunday. In other days the *thyajyam* has no significance.

2. Chandrashtama shows no evil when the Moon is waxing and occupies a benefic sign and a benefic Navamsa, or when there is Tarabala. The sting is lost when the Moon and the 8th lord are friends.

3. Tuesday is not evil after midday.

4. The aspects attributed to Vyatipatam, Vaidruti, etc., become defunct after midday.

5. No day of the week is blemished if the lord thereof is strongly placed in the election chart.

6. Venus, Mercury or Jupiter in the ascendant will completely destroy all other adverse influences.

7. Jupiter has the power of dispelling all the evils due to the Lagna, Navamsa and malefic aspects and render the time highly propitious.

8. The mere presence of the Moon or the Sun in the 11th will act as an antidote for other evils obtaining in the horoscope.

9. If the angles are well fortified, evil influences are countered.

10. A planet exalted in Lagna will nullify the other adverse influences.

11. Jupiter or Venus in a kendra (quadrant) and malefics in 3, 6 or 11 will remove all the flaws arising on account of unfavourable weekday, constellation, lunar day and yoga.

Thus it will be seen that the most important question in Muhurtha is the fortification of Lagna and its lord.

CHAPTER VI

On Certain Special Yogas

When a certain weekday coincides with a certain asterism and a certain lunar day, it becomes specially auspicious for good work. In this chapter, I shall give a few such special combinations which go under the special distinction of Siddha Yogas.

Sunday coinciding with the 1st, 4th, 6th, 7th or 12th lunar day and ruled by the constellations Pushya, Hasta, Uttara, Uttarashadha, Moola, Sravana or Uttarabhadra gives rise to Siddha Yoga.

Monday identical with the 2nd, 7th or 12th lunar day and with the constellations Rohini, Mrigasira, Punarvasu, Chitta, Sravana, Satabhisha, Dhanishta or Poorvabhadra produces the same yoga.

Tuesday falling on a day ruled by Aswini, Mrigasira, Chitta, Anuradha, Moola, Uttara, Dhanishta or Poorvabhadra gives rise to Siddha Yoga.

Wednesday coinciding with Bhadra and Jaya and with the constellations Rohini, Mrigasira, Aridra, Uttara, Uttarashadha or Anuradha generates Siddha Yoga.

Thursday identical with the 4th, 5th, 7th, 9th, 13th or 14th lunar day and with the asterisms Makha, Pushya, Punarvasu, Swati, Poorvashadha, Poorvabhadra, Revati or Aswini gives rise to Siddha Yoga.

Friday ruled by Aswini, Bharani, Aridra, Uttara,

Chitta, Swati, Poorvashadha or Revati coinciding with Nanda and Bhadra constitutes this beneficial yoga.

Saturday falling on a day ruled by Swati, Rohini, Visakha, Anuradha, Dhanishta or Satabhisha and with lunar days Bhadra and Riktha generates the same auspicious yoga.

A Friday coinciding with Nanda (1st, 6th and 11th lunar days), Wednesday identical with Bhadra (2nd, 7th and 12th lunar days), Tuesday coinciding with Jaya (3rd 8th and 13th lunar days), Saturday falling on a Riktha tithi (4th, 9th and 14th lunar days), and Thursday falling on 5th, 10th or 15th (Poorna) lunar days constitute Siddha Yoga.

Sunday to Saturday respectively coinciding with the constellations Hasta, Sravana, Aswini, Anuradha, Pushya, Revati and Rohini will give rise to Amita Siddha Yoga.

The above special yogas can be applied with advantage to important elections and if in addition to the general strength of the day due to a special yoga, the Lagna is also rendered strong, chances of success of the enterprise would be by far the greatest.

CHAPTER VII

Pre-Natal Ceremonies

Before the actual birth of a child, three important ceremonies are enjoined to be performed. They are nuptials (Nisheka), consummation (Garbhadana) and Pumsavana (change of sex).

Nisheka is used to denote the first sexual contact, while Garbhadana has reference to the subsequent deflorations. Almost all the ancient works on Muhurtha start from Namakarana—the name-giving ceremony after the birth of a child—but we start from consummation as it is actually the beginning of the pre-natal existence of the child. Sexual union, pregnancy and reproduction of human species are the essentials on which the world exists. Sexual union should never be based upon simple sense gratification. There is a sacredness about sexual functions, and when moral and spiritual considerations are not respected and brought into play, the result will be most unsatisfactory and all sorts of undesirable progeny would be the products of promiscuous cohabitation. According to Prof. B. Suryanarain Rao men and women are bundles of electricity. When they are brought together sexually a series of electrical currents would be released which may react on them favourably or adversely depending upon the harmonious or discordant nature of the vibrations released. Therefore the first sexual act should not be treated lightly and should be done only when planetary combinations are favourably disposed. Books on ancient Sexology and Astrology reveal that to indulge in coitus during the first four days of menses will lead to serious evil effects as the whole physiological and nervous system of the woman would be in a state of tension owing to the almost continuous discharge of blood. So the first four days of menses should be avoided. Copulation on the 5th day tends to give rise to a daughter. In general, sexual union on odd days indicates birth of female children while on even days, the birth of male children is indicated. In the first instance, sexual union is highly recommended on the 6th day of the menses as it is supposed to ensure not only happiness to the couple but also the birth of a dutiful and intelligent son.

The constellations Sravana, Rohini, Anuradha, Swati, Revati, Moola, Uttara, Uttarashadha, Uttarabhadra, Satabhisha are highly favourable for nuptials. Pushyami, Dhanishta, Mrigasira, Aswini, Chitta, Punarvasu are ordinary. The rest of constellations are to be rejected.

Monday, Wednesday, Thursday and Friday are auspicious days while Saturday, Tuesday and Sunday should not be considered at all.

All lunar days except the 4th, 8th, 9th, 14th, Full Moon and New Moon are good. The favourable signs are Taurus to Libra and Pisces. The birth star (Janma Nakshatra), the 10th star (Anu Janma) and the 19th star (Thri Janma) should be avoided.

At the time of nuptials, the 8th house should be occupied by no planet. Subject to this proviso, even Sagittarius and Aquarius may be selected as auspicious.

Pumsavana.—This means change of sex. The Hindus had long ago known the processes whereby the sex of the foetus could be changed by performing certain remedies and by administering certain medicines when sex differentiation is about to set in. The possibility of change of sex long known to the Hindus was being ridiculed by Western scientists. But during the last 3 or 4 decades, the opinion of the scientists underwent a gradual change and most of them now admit such a possibility. For the information of the reader, I may just make a few observations of modern medical men on this all-important question.

Professor Thury first started a theory about the possibility of changing the sex of the foetus in the womb. This was taken up by Professor Unterberger. Bernard Macfadden has reached certain conclusions regarding the predetermination of the sex with a success claimed in 90 per cent of cases experimented. According to the theory of Thury "the biogenetic condition, prevailing in the female organism in the beginning of the interval between two menstrual periods is favourable to girls. Towards the end of this interval, shortly before the new period, it is favourable to boys. In between, the chances are even". It is possible that the chemistry of the mother undergoes natural changes at certain times which correspond to the condition of alkalinity on acidity created artificially by Unterberger with the aid of bicarbonate or lactic acid.

There are, according to Davenport, probably four hundred theories of sex determination promulgated during the last two or three hundred years. One theory generally accepted by biologists maintains that sex is determined by the so called X chromosomes. In the female there are two of these chromosomes. In the male there is only one. Professor Blchm suggested that the male chromosomes move more quickly in alkaline solution than the chromosomes which carry the feminine principle.

A teaspoonful of bicarbonate of soda or one spoonful of lactic acid may thus determine the sex of the child. Generally 105 boys are born for every 100 girls. The mortality among the boys is somewhat greater. It has been found that after great and destructive wars, where men are killed on a large scale, the number of male births increases. Nature thus restores the balance of sexes. We have known parents, some of them longing for girls while others want boys for keeping up their family traditions and for continuance of their lines. This will be so specially in cases of inheritance and succession to thrones and large landed and financial estates. Many wars and bloodshed were the results of kings and queens having no sons to succeed them. In almost all the countries the dynasties were kept up through sons. Matriarchy forms an exception.

It was found out by experiment that a high acid secretion was frequently responsible for sterility in the female. When douche were applied in the form of sodium bicarbonate, where there were no pathological changes in either husband or wife the results were most gratifying. The pregnancy developed after the next period and in every case the child was a boy. Professor Unterberger observes "that the most important thing appears to be the fact that the characteristics of the female organs exercise a great influence on the determination of the sex which strange to say has been ignored heretofore". Professor Nicolai Konstantinovitch of Moscow discovered an electric treatment which separates and segregates the male and female spermatozoa. It is said that children of either sex may be obtained by using chromosomes of the opposite sex in artificial impregnation. Natural spermatozoa are deposited in the curved end of the tube filled with a physiological solution. A slight electrical current draws the male and female cells opposite ends of the tubes. The male spermatozoa are drawn to the anodes or the side where the current enters the tube, and the female sperms to the cathodes, where the current leaves. Macfadden says "conception time with reference to the menstrual cycle normally runs its course in twenty-eight days and so corresponds in length to the lunar month".

Here is a feminine physiological habit which in some ways at present clearly understood closely corresponds to the movements of the Moon. The theory is, that if fertilised when first discharged from the ovary the ovum is female in tendency while later as the ovum ages it becomes male, so that fertilisation between the 3rd and the 5th days after menstruation is liable to produce a girl, between the 5th and 8th days, a boy or a girl, and between the 8th and 12th days a boy. We have evidence that certain physiological habits curiously correspond to the lunar daily cycles even as the habit of the menstruation, a sex function corresponds to the lunar monthly cycle.

It has been suggested by the mighty Darwin that since life apparently originated on the beaches of primordial sea where it was alternately covered and uncovered by the tides, through countless ages, certain life rhythms and physiological habits were formed in all living creatures to correspond with those tidal rhythms, which in their turn were regulated by the Sun and the Moon. The primitive cell, which was the cradle of the life-force, at that time went through alternating period of activity and quiescence. The scientific name for these two physiological phases is Katabolism and Anabolism. Physiologically Anabolism and Katabolism correspond to maleness and femaleness. These facts lead to some interesting conclusions about sex as possibly determined not merely by the time of the lunar month, but by the time of the lunar day at which conception takes place. Here all the greatest scientists on matters of conception and sex formation are agreed on the physiological effects of cycles of lunar days and lunar months.

We shall now quote from our astrological literature, what they have unanimously said about the appearances of menses, how the foetus develops in the womb, in what month the sex is formed, how the sex of the unborn child in the womb can be known and by what methods the sex of the child may be changed as per desire of the parents.

Occassionally one reads in papers about the reversal or change of sex to a certain degree even in adults. This phenomenon has been actually witnessed by Prof. B. Suryanarain Rao and of late it is becoming common. In the history of science the ancient Hindus occupy a foremost place because thousands of years ago, they had anticipated and in fact achieved what to the moderns appear as marvels of biology. Of course, it is a fashion with those who have received the European system of education of laugh at things they cannot explain with the aid of their own pet theories.

Charaka, the great Hindu physician, has dwelt at length with the question of change of sex. The ancients had not only studied the theory but they have given us practical rules whereby the sex of the unborn child in the womb may be known in advance and changed, if so desired. Ceremonies are actually laid down in the Vedas for performance by the father and the mother with a view to give the child in the womb the sex that is desired. These rites are called *pumsavana*. The etymology of the word is: *pung* (male) *syate* (is produced) *anena* (by this) ; in other words the male-producing rite. These rites are performed even unto this day by every orthodox Hindu. *Pumsavana* is performed just after the expiration of three months from date of conception.

Before giving further details about *Pumsavana* let us bring to the attention of the readers an interesting phenomenon which recently happened in Europe. Andreas Sparre, a Danish painter, married at the age of 20, a student artist studying in a like academy as his in Paris. They had a happy life for some time. A few years later Andreas Sparre happened to dress up in fun as a woman. The clothes suited him and he looked like a girl. One of his friends called him Lili and he liked this name. Soon afterwards Andreas began to feel that Lili was after all a real individual—a separate personality, existing within himself. Gradually, this second personality pushed to the background, his maleness. Andreas experienced bleeding from the mouth and nose and this was regarded as a form of menstruation. Of course there was a psychological change too that he was becoming more and more feminine. With the passing of time a conviction grew in his mind that though male in his outward form, internally he possessed the female sexual organs. Physicians and surgeons whom he consulted could not offer any explanation for his dual personality. At last he consulted a German specialist who declared after a careful examination that Andreas possessed female sexual organs within himself. After this he was operated upon by Prof Gebherd and after the operation the attending nurses remarked to Andreas that his voice had completely changed and that it was a shrill woman's voice. Then cigarettes and cigars nauseated him and even his handwriting turned feminine. In this first operation the male-sex glands were completely removed and Andreas Sparre was no longer a man. After the second operation Grete, the wife of Andreas, wrote as follows in her diary:—

"Not until a few hours later did I learn what had happened inside—a human being who was born a man, who was my husband, my friend, my comrade had now become a woman, a complete woman."

"But the thought which haunts me is that though Andreas may now be extinguished, and though Lili may have risen like a phoenix from the ashes, yet in the world outside Andreas is still living in the eyes of the law, and I am his wife. Who is capable of grasping this horror, this fantastic idea, this unique happening."

What are we to think of this strange and tragic case of Andhreas Sparre—a case unique in medical history. The case of *Obalamma* becoming *Obalachari* (vide *Female Horoscopy* by Prof. B. Suryanarain Rao) is also equally interesting.

Though medically it is impossible to distinguish sex in the embryo, astrologically it is possible to know beforehand—based on the conception Lagna—whether the child would be male or female. Doctors also opine that even in the most normal and unambiguous individual the rudiments of the organs of the other sex are present throughout life. *Pumsavana* means not only rites but also administering of certain medicines. Who knows, the proper performance of *Pumsavana* may enable us to change sexes of even adults, because the medicines accompanied by mantras may act on the glandular secretions and change the very nature of such secretion. The cases of Andreas and Obalamma suggest that change of sex is possible and that ancient Hindus when they talked of this phenomenon were not merely guessing but were treading on solid and scientific grounds.

A persual of the various texts in Sanskrit bearing on astrology and medicine reveals that *Pumsavana* is closely connected with the planetary influences on embroynic development. All the phases of the union of the virile spermatozoan with the mature ovum called impregnation, the fixation of the impregnated ovum, called conception, and the development of the foetus are governed by the Moon and other planets.

No birth takes place by chance. In most cases, impregnation follows very shortly after coitus and it is the time of coitus that is generally taken according to Hindu Astrology for the *Nisheka* or conception horoscope. The period of gestation is the time which elapses between the conception and partruition, during which the child first as embryo, then as foetus is developing in the womb. Beginning with the third week, the head bend in the embryo is quite marked which gradually increases as development goes on, and at the end of the third week the heart and all the organs have been laid down and limbs begin to make their appearance as small buds, not unlike those of the frog, and the embryo closely resembles any other mammalian embryo at a corresponding stage. The chief changes in the first month (governed of course by Venus) are the formation of the face and external ear, and the development of the limbs. The eyes, nasal pits, maxillary processes, ears and nose are now visible.

In the second month of pregnancy—ruled by Mars— the plasm is enveloped by the amnion. Mars brings the development of the membranes and strong expansion of them. The brain begins to develop, the head becomes considerably larger and the human characters are all established. The embryo may now be spoken of as the foetus, which has passed its quadruped stage.

Now we come to the third month influenced largely by Jupiter—the month in which *Pumsavana* has to be performed if one desires to have a son born to him. *It is in the third month the differentiation of sex is brought about*, as also the development of the genitals. Jupiter a masculine planet, presides over this month. Thus it will be seen that in the selection of the time for performing *Pumsavana* the ancients had in view very scientific reasons. As difference of sex occurs in the third month, the medicines and mantras administered under the influence of certain constellations would certainly be capable enough to change the sex to the desire of the individual concerned. Without caring to bestow serious thought on such questions, the moderner is apt to dismiss the whole thing as the product of superstition.

We shall now give a few hints from the famous *Charaka Samhita* and it is for readers to make use of such hints to their own advantage.

Charaka says: "Instructions will be laid down about those Vedic rites by which the sex of the child (in the womb) before its *manifestation* may be changed. Verily of rites duly performed and *characterised by propriety of time and place,* the capacity to produce desirable fruits is ordained. Observing that a woman has concieved, *Pumsavana* should be administered to her before the manifestation of the sex of the child in the womb.

"Obtaining two unbroken buds from two twigs procured from the eastern and northern sides of a banian (*Picus indica*, Linn.) growing in a cowpen, as also a single grain of paddy and a single seed of *Masha Phaseolus radiatus* Roxb.) both well developed, or two seeds of white mustard, and throwing them into a quantity of curds, the woman (that has concieved) should be made to drink it under the constellation of Pushya." Another *Pumsavanam* medicine is the following :—

The *kalka* or paste of (*a*) *jeevaka*,[1] (*b*) *rishabhaka*,[2] (*c*) *Apamarga*[3] or (*d*) *Sahachara*[4] or of each if desirable— should be boiled with milk and given to the woman to drink.

"Or, the likeness of a man, or very small proportions, made of gold, or silver or iron, made red-hot in fire and then dipped into a measure of curds, or milk, or water, should be swallowed without leaving any remnant, under the influence of the constellation *Pushyami*. Under the same nakshatra of Pushymi, the woman may be made to inhale the hot vapour of a cake (*pishta* or *pishtaka*) that is being baked (on the fire) and then dissolving that cake in a measure of water, the mixture should be cast over the threshold of the door. This water the woman should then, using a stick of cotton, apply to her right nostril."

If the above remedies are administered under the favourable and auspicious influences of constellation, the sex in the womb of the woman is supposed to change. The subject is vast and we shall again recur to this on a subsequent occasion. Who has studied and who has tested all these methods ? Why label them as useless and unscientific when you do not know that they are.

The ceremony of *Pumsavanam* should be celebrated in the 3rd month when signs of pregnancy are evident.

---

1. Jeevaka is no longer identifiable or procurable. Hindu doctors find substitute in *Guduchi* or *Tinospora cordifolia*, Miqs.
2. This is also not identifiable. The substitute is *Vanggalochana* or bamboo manna.
3. *Achyaranthes*, Linn.
4. *Barlenia cristata*, Linn.

All lunar days except the 4th, 6th, 8th, 9th, 12th, 14th, Full Moon and New Moon days are good.

All signs except Gemini, Cancer and Virgo are auspicious. Virgo should be avoided as it is specially adverse.

Monday, Wednesday, Thursday and Friday are beneficial. The 8th house from the ascendant should be vacant. The Moon's presence in Lagna or the 12th and the ascendant being aspected by Venus brings on prosperity. Benefics should be disposed in quadrants or trines.

There is another ceremony named Seemantha immediately following *Pumsavanam*, being performed in the 5th or 7th month of pregnancy. This is ordained only in regard to first conceptions. If the time-schedule cannot be kept up, it should not be abandoned, but the function must be performed at least before delivery. This is the view of sage Sankha.

For Seemantha, Rohini, Mrigasira, Punarvasu, Pushyami, Uttara, Uttarashadha, Hasta, Sravana and Revati are auspicious. Some are of the opinion that under unavoidable circumstances, even Aswini, Anuradha and Moola may be deemed auspicious. The 4th, 6th, 8th 9th, 14th lunar days and New Moon day must be avoided. When the Moon is dignified Full Moon day is not condemned. Sunday, Tuesday and Saturday should be avoided. The rest of the weekdays are good. All signs except Leo and Scorpio are auspicious. The 8th house from the ascendant must be free. Generally speaking, the 3rd, 5th, 7th, 10th and 22nd constellations should be avoided. The Moon should not be in the 8th house. So far as this particular ceremony is concerned, the month ranks first in importance. Hence, even if Jupiter and Venus are combust, such a circumstance may be ignored.

CHAPTER VIII

Post-Natal Ceremonies

Namakarana or naming the child.—The proper day for this ceremony would be the 10th, 12th or 16th day of the child's birth. If this is not possible, then an auspicious day must be fixed for the purpose.

Anuradha, Punarvasu, Makha, Uttara, Uttarashadha, Uttarabhadra, Satabhisha, Swati, Dhanishta, Sravana, Rohini, Aswini, Mrigasira, Revati, Hasta and Pushya are auspicious.

The 4th, 6th, 8th, 9th, 12th, 14th lunar days, Full Moon and New Moon should be avoided.

Monday, Wednesday, Thursday and Friday are good. Other weekdays are not good. As far as possible, the Lagna must be rendered strong and the 8th house should be unoccupied. Fixed signs are preferable and common signs are good when occupied by benefics.

If Jupiter occupies a kendra or thrikona and a malefic is in the 11th, the time is held to be very auspicious. Another equally propitious combination is the time when the Lagna falls in a benefic sign with a malefic in the 3rd, Venus in 12th and the Moon in a dignified position.

Generally the name to be given to a male child should consist of an even number of letters (*e.g.*, Rama, Krishna, etc.), while a female child should be given a name containing uneven number of letters *e.g.*, Parvati,

Janaki, etc.). The name must also be appropriate to the ruling star.

Cradling.—The best time for this would be the 10th, 12th, 16th, or the 22nd day after its birth.

First Feeding on Rice (*Annaprasana*).—Let the first feeding on rice be done in the 6th, 8th, 9th, or 12th month on days ruled by Aswini, Mrigasira, Punarvasu, Dhanishta, Pushyami, Hasta, Swati, Anuradha, Sravana, Satabhisha, Uttara, and Chitta, avoiding the usual unfavourable lunar days. The 10th house must be unoccupied. The first feeding should not be done in the constellation of Aridra, Krittika, Jyeshta, Bharani, Aslesha, Poorvashadha and Poorvabhadra.

Monday, Wednesday, Thursday and Friday are good. Aries, Scorpio and Pisces are inauspicious. Mercury, Mars and Venus should not occupy respectively the 7th, 8th and 9th houses. Mercury, Jupiter or Venus in Lagna is highly commendable. No malefic should occupy the ascendant.

The most important factor in this function is the month; hence one should not mind even if Jupiter and Venus are combust.

Ear Boring (*Karnavedha*).—This should be done on the 12th of 16th day of the birth of the child or in the 6th, 7th or 8th month, either in the forenoon or in the afternoon but never during night. A day ruled by two asterisms or two lunar days is not propitious as also the other lunar days usually declared as inauspicious.

Monday, Wednesday, Thursday and Friday are good. At the time of boring the ears, the 8th house should be unoccupied. Aquarius, Leo and Scorpio should be rejected.

Tonsure (*Chowlam*).—The learned say that Chowlam is a very important karma because it involves the first cutting of hair which means discharge of electrical currents from the child for the first time. The ceremony when properly done is said to prolong the life of the child. It should not be done when the mother of the child is pregnant. Chowlam may be performed in the 3rd or 5th year when Jupiter and Venus are free from combustion and when the Sun is in the Tropic of Cancer. The bright fortnight is said to give longevity while the dark fortnight is supposed to affect the health.

The 2nd, 3rd, 5th, 7th, 10th, 11th and 13th lunar days are good. The 4th, 1st, 6th, 8th, 9th 14th and New and Full Moon days should be rejected.

Punarvasu, Mrigasira, Dhanishta, Sravana, Revati Pushya, Chitta, Aswini, Hasta are favourable; Swati, Rohini, Satabhisha, Uttara, Uttarabhadra, Uttarashadha are ordinary. Tonsure should always be done in the forenoon.

Monday, Wednesday, Thursday and Friday are good.

Cancer, Virgo, Gemini, Pisces, Libra, Taurus and Capricorn rising give rise to good results. The rest are not beneficial. But they can be employed provided benefics occupy the Lagna and the Lagna is otherwise strong. But Aquarius should be rejected at any cost, no matter how powerful it might be. Let the benefics occupy the 4th, 5th, 7th, 9th, 10th and 11th and malefics the 3rd, 6th and 11th. The 8th house must remain unoccupied. The 7th house should not be occupied by either the Sun or Mars or preferably by any malefic.

Commencing Education (Aksharabhyasa).—Alphabet is a crude translation of the word 'Akshara'. Akshara means that which cannot be destroyed and therefore akshara simply indestructible forms of sound vibrations.

When such sound vibrations are first put into the child's ears, they must be such as to give the child a good chance of calling out the latent energies in him or her so that the course of training may run smoothly and to his best advantage.

The most propitious period for commencing education is the 5th day in the 5th month of the 5th year. The following days constellations are good: Monday, Wednesday, Thursday and Friday; Aswini, Punarvasu, Aridra, Hasta, Chitta, Swati, Sravana and Revati.

Movable and common signs are good.

Forenoon and noon are preferable. The 8th house should be unoccupied.

Mercury, Venus, Jupiter in the 9th counteracts all evil influences.

Investiture of Sacred Thread (Upanayanam).—*This is a ceremony in which spiritiual instructions are given by authorised persons to give spiritual eye to the boy by which his internal vision is brought closer to the Universal light or God. This ceremony is peculiar to the Hindus. But as the name indicates, any section of the human society, whether Hindu or not, may take advantage of these valuable precepts and begin to give their children the religious instruction most suitable to their countries, castes and traditions. Upanayanam should be performed in the 5th or the 8th year. If this is not possible, the ceremoney should be gone through before the age of 16 in case of Brahmins and 20 to 24 in regard to other sects of the Hindus.

The Sun, the Moon and Jupiter represent symbolically the father, mother and life-force. Therefore, the three planets should be well disposed to the ascendant at the time of Upanayanam.

The best season is when the Sun is in his northern course (between Capricorn and Gemini). The lunar

---
* Prof. B. Suryanarain Rao's *Sukla and Promoduta*.

months of Magha, Phalguna, Chaitra and Vaisakha are good. The 2nd, 3rd, 5th, 7th, 10th and 13th lunar days in the bright half and the 1st, 2nd and 3rd in the dark half are held to be auspicious. The lunar days to be avoided are 4th, 8th, 9th, 11th, 12th, 14th and Full and New Moon days. Some are of opinion that the 13th is good.

Exception : Even the 14th lunar day may be treated as good if the boy is above the prescribed age.

Monday, Wednesday, Thursday and Friday are propitious. Wednesday must be rejected if Mercury is combust. Sunday is ordinary while Tuesday should be invariably rejected.

The following constellations are good : Anuradha, Hasta, Chitta, Swati, Sravana, Dhanishta, Satabhisha, Uttara, Uttarashadha, Uttarabhadra, Revati, Rohini, Mrigasira, Aswini, Punarvasu and Pushyami.

Aries, Taurus, Gemini, Cancer, Virgo, Libra and Aquarius are good. The other signs should be avoided. According to Vasishta and Garga, the 3rd day in the bright half of the month of Chaitra and Vaisakha and the 7th day in the bright half of the lunar months Magha and Phalguna are highly favourable.

The Moon must not occupy the 6th, 8th, or 12th house. Malefics should not be posited in quadrants. The ceremony should take place before noon. The 8th house from the Lagna must be unoccupied.

The third house should be fortified by the situation of either malefics or benefics, while the 6th should be devoid of a benefic. Mars and Saturn should be avoided in the 5th.

Let Mars and Saturn be avoided in the 2nd from the election chart ; as otherwise they will make the boy's intellect dull. Similarly their situation in the 12th should also be avoided. The Moon should always be avoided in Lagna. But, however, if Cancer is the ascendant and the Moon and Jupiter are in conjunction and malefics are in 3, 6 and 11, the evil attached to the situation of the Moon in Lagna becomes neutralised. The following malefic yogas should also be avoided:

Spoorjitham.—The Sun in kendra causes this yoga and the result is the destruction of the family.

Spuritham.—Mars occupying a kendra generates this evil yoga and generally proves fatal to the Guru (preceptor) as well as the boy.

Rudhitham.—Saturn occupying a kendra produces this evil combination resulting in incurable diseases.

Rundhram.—Rahu in a kendra gives rise to this malefic yoga. It proves fatal to the mother.

Ugram.—This arises by Ketu's disposition in a kendra. It adversely affects health and education.

Besides the above malefic yogas, the Moon should not be affected by Mercury as it leads to the boy's blindness. The Moon should not be in her own Navamsa, nor in that of the Sun or Mars.

The following are of course very favourable combinations for Upanayanam:

(1) The 6th, 7th or 8th house from the Moon being occupied by a benefic.

(2) The Sun or Venus in the 12th, Mercury in the 2nd and Jupiter in a trine or a quadrant.

(3) Venus in Lagna, Mercury in the 10th, the Sun in the 11th and the Moon in a benefic navamsa.

(4) When the Lagna is Pisces occupied by Jupiter or Venus with the Sun in the 11th and Mercury in the 10th or 12th house.

(5) Gemini rising with Mars in Aries, Venus in Taurus and the Moon in Cancer.

CHAPTER XI

Marriage

Marriage is a most complicated structure made up as it is of a whole series of subjective and objective facts of a very heterogeneous nature. Since we are concerned with the psycho-astrological aspect of marriage we shall exclude the objective factors of legal and social nature although these factors have a pronounced influence on the psychological relationship of the married pair.

Marriage is not an institution for simple brute sense gratification. The idea that it is a civil contract terminable at will smacks of meanness in conception of the grand liabilities and assets between the parties to be engaged in sacred wedlock. One of the great American judges said "the contract of marriage is something more than a civil agreement between the parties, the extent of which only affects themselves. It is the basis of the family, and its dissolution as well as its formation is a matter of public policy in which the body or community is deeply interested and it is to be governed by other considerations than those which obtain with regard to any other civil contract that the ground which shall invalidate the contract must be something more than a mere representation as to collateral matters that no ground will annul a marriage which does not go to the very essence of the contract".

Marriage, both in the social and economic sense, is a sexual relationship entered into with the intention of making it permanent. In India, marriage was and is regarded as a religious sacrament and marriage comprehends the equality of the partner in respect of Dharma (right conduct), Artha (financial position,) Karma (sex relation) and Moksha (final salvation). The universality of marriage constitutes one of the most striking differences between the Hindus and the other races. When the question of marriage is considered, various factors demand our attention, important ones being physical fitness, mental qualities, heredity, sexual compatibility and social and economic status.

In the modren world so much is made of the sex element in marriage that the other equally important factors, social and psychological, are practically ignored. The Hindu Sastras, having in view the climatic and ethnological conditions of India, have fixed the maximum and minimum age limits for marriage. Marriages between parties belonging to the same Gotra are not favoured perhaps because of the dysgenic influence on the offspring. Inter-racial, intercommunal and inter-religious marriages are not looked upon favourably because in such matches there are cultural differences.

After a careful consideration of all these factors, the Hindus had devised an astrological means of judging marriage compatibility whereby the relations between the couple may stand the strain of maladjustments. Pseudo-sexologists and sociologists are not wanting in India who are ever ready to point out their finger of contempt at the sound and sensible institution of marriage developed by the Hindus after centuries of experience and experiments. We are not concerned with such socialistic theories advocating companionate marriage and encouraging unbridled licence in love affairs. They may be all right in countries like Russia and America—the melting pots of different races. But they cannot hold water in a country like India whose civilsation, culture and social laws are peculiar to her geographical and historical positions.

The Hindus have solved this complex problem of marriage selection by recourse to astrological considerations. If investigations into the various *kutas* are undertaken before the marriage is contracted, there will perhaps be fewer tragedies than at present and less marital infidelity. Modern science has devised no means to find out the compatibility between the marrying couple. Sexologists suggest that the bride and bridegroom should subject themselves to a thorough medical examination. Although this sounds reasonable, it makes an important omission in that mere physical fitness does not ensure complete marital happiness. Happiness largely rests upon so many other factors that the aid of astrology should be sought for by every sensible individual.

In selecting horoscopes for marriage purposes, three factors have to be carefully considered. They are :—

(*a*) The longevity of the bride and the bridegroom.

(*b*) The larger strength of the 7th and 8th houses.

(*c*) Agreeability in regard to the Kutas or pooruththam.

When there is no longevity in the case of bride, the horoscope must be rejected even though the 7th house may be strong or the requsite number of units are available. Likewise when the 7th house is weak and is considerably blemished, the horoscope to be matched should have antidotes or counteracting influences.

The kutas or the units of agreement should be considered only when there is general sympathy between the horoscopes of the parties to be brought together. The existing practice almost all over India and particularly in the South is highly defective and dangerous as horoscopes are rejected simply because they do not conform to certain kutas, while the most important factors such as longevity, widowhood, etc., are completely ignored.

Therefore it is very essential to examine to start with, the general strength of the chart; and when good longevity is indicated in both horoscopes and they are free from the afflictions in regard to the 7th and 8th houses, further agreement should be judged. When Mars and Venus are in the 7th, the boy or girl concerned will have strong sex-instincts and such an individual should be mated to one who has similar instincts and not a person having Mercury or Jupiter in the 7th, as this makes one under-sexed. When sexual incompatibility sets in marriage, life proves charmless and friction arises between the couple. Therefore it is the duty of the parents to consult learned astrologers and not to entrust the work of comparing horoscopes to all persons who have no practical experience. History is replete with ill-matched marriages and the most miserable lives the couples had to live.

Socrates philosopher as he was reputed to be, was united in marriage to Xantippe who, if rightly reported, perpetually ridiculed his philosophical teachings and mercilessy nagged him in his home. Once when he had invited a distinguished friend to dinner, she spitefully emptied the contents of a vessel upon his head. Plato sympathisingly asked him why he bore such indignities. Meekly replied the old philosopher: "She teaches me patience and charity, and shows to me that if I can bear with her, I can bear all else in the world". Alcibiades, noted for brilliancy of intellect and a most graceful carriage of personality, was strangely unfortunate in his marital relations. Too proud to directly desert his wife he at one time contemplated and even attempted suicide as a release from his bonds.

Pericles, ruling Athens for 50 years, finding it brick and leaving it marble, was not only orator and statesman, but in other ways the most discrete and majestic character of that remote period. His relations with Aspasia caused bitterest criticism. His wife, being a fault finding social drag, failing to stand by him supporting him in his great work for the upholding of Athens, he deliberately parted with her, bestowing upon her half of his estates.

Plato, warned by Socrates, his teacher, though noble, wealthy, scholastic and exceedingly popular in the higher walks of Grecian society never married, though a great admirer and lover of women.

Cicero, the Roman orator and early pleader in the forum, studied at the feet of Zeno and Demetrius and married the heiress Terentia.

It is needless to produce the full story of his unsatisfactory married life. Milton, holding in English literature one of the highest places as poet and patriot, wrote three pamphlets upon divorce and lived not merely unhappily but at times miserably with his wife, Mary Powell.

Thomas Carlyle's married life was rough as a tempestuous sea and accordingly far from being happy. Dickens, as writer, author and world painter of human emotions, stood for a time in Great Britain unrivalled and yet his matrimonial home life was a most painful failure.

We can multiply the instances any number. In the modern times, America counts such social shipwrecks by thousands upon thousands both in the lower and the higher planes of marital life. In India also the number is on the increase. All these tell their own sad stories of connubial dissatisfaction and family wretchedness. Readers must note that in the examples given above, the married lives were not shattered by the death of wife, or husband but they proved tragic because of the dislike between husband and wife.

Having read the above paragraphs, the reader may be tempted to put the question "Is marriage—true harmonial marriage—possible at the present state of the world's civilisation?" The quick answer is in the affirmative.

A careful consideration of the important astrological works reveals the following information :—

(1) If Kuja is in the 7th house unaspected or not joined by benefics, there will be frequent quarrels in the married life often leading to misunderstandings and separation.

(2) When Saturn is in the 8th house, and particularly in a square to Mars, the married life will be crossed by discord, lack of mutual understanding and want of real attachment.

(3) When Leo is Lagna and the 7th lord Saturn is in the 2nd, the husband will be subservient to the wife carrying out all her orders.

(4) Saturn in the 7th house is also indicative of unhappiness in marriage unless Saturn happens to be either lord of Lagna or lord of the 7th.

(5) According to *Prasna Marga*, the famous Kerala work on Astrology, if the Sun and Venus occupy the 5th,

---

* See English translation of *Prasna Marga* by Dr. B. V. Raman.

7th, or 9th house then the native will lack marital happiness.

(6) A strong malefic in the 4th, particularly Mars, is not conducive to conjugal happiness.

(7) If in the *Ashtakavarga* of Venus, the 7th house from Venus contains a large number of bindus (positive units) and the wife is born in any of the asterisms of the Sun, then his wife will be as dear to him as life.

(8) When the longitude of the 7th house falls in a malefic Navamsa, frequent quarrels and misunderstandings will ensue.

(9) If the lords of the 7th and 1st are friends then the native will be loved by his wife. Otherwise there will be no harmony.

The above combinations do not speak of either the death of wife or more than one marriage. They simply state that the dispositions of planets in a certain manner in the (male's or female's) horoscope, render the marital life unhappy.

(10) Make the necessary reductions in the *Ashtakavarga** of Venus. Mark those signs that contain bindus or dots. Then take that sign which contains more dots and get the bride from the direction indicated by that sign. The marriage is said to bring real happiness.

We should like to make a few observations based on our studies and experience.

Today in the Western countries, one in every three marriages is said to end in divorce. Love, affection and loyalty appear to be inconsistent or out of date with a gadget-geared, money-mad and permissive society. During our last visit to U.S., Mrs. X who drove us from Washington to New York narrated her tale, which is briefly as follows :—A lawyer by profession, Mrs. X, 28,

---

* *Ashtakavarga System of Prediction* by Dr. B. V. Raman.

had married another lawyer, after "knowing him well" and had a son from him. Two years of their married life crossed by frequent quarrels, "temperamental clashes", etc., resulted in divorce proceedings. The possession of the child was given by the court to the father. The mother Mrs. X revolted and she became miserable. She was seeking astrological advice whether she could marry another attorney who was in similar predicament having divorced his first wife.

This case is typical of many American marriages. Mrs. X had met an Indian lady and had been astonished to learn that in India most marriages "were arranged" by the parents and that the very idea of divorce was still repugnant to the average Indian lady. And she was also told that astrology played a vital role in the selection of parents; all of which astonished her so much that she began to study astrology and "felt convinced" that Indian Society had certain in-built safety valves which made marriages stable; and that despite the free mixing of sexes and the permissive nature of man-woman relations in the West, astrology could be of immense value in the selection of brides and bridegrooms, so that the incidence of divorce could be reduced to some extent.

Thanks to the intellectual slavery of the Indians some of the "progressives" are now clamouring for the introduction of sex-education in schools and colleges in India blindly aping the Westerners and unmindful of the jeopardising of the moral basis and sancitity of man and woman relations.

Paradoxically it is now being felt in many Western countries that the so-called sex education instead of being "enlightening" by way of imparting "scientific truths" and "natural biological functions" is completely deviod of moral guidance and has resulted in an improper sensationalistic approach on the part of young students, because sex is viewed from the Freudian point of view as mere biological function and not from the Jungian point of view, as a vital force capable of being directed through creative channels.

Today the tragedy of India appears to be that Indian people are to be considered as guinea pigs for experimenting with theories, once fashionable in the west, and now being increasingly rejected as adversely influencing the stability of marriage and family life.

Recently an enterprising Indian scholar had a German professor of Sociology as his guest. The German professor remarked that he found the institution of marriage much more of a success in India and that he could feel the presence of deeper harmony in domestic relations in India than in any other civilised region he had so far visited.

The Indian professor's reply was that this stability and harmony were probably due to the system of martrimonial matching of horoscopes, invariably resorted to by parents prior to the settling of marriages. The Indian scholar started collecting case histories of married couples and he managed to get 603 cases for study. The age group selected was 30 to 40. All the people concerned were born between 1931-40 and married between 1955-60. The economic background was mostly rural and agricultural though 22% of the case histories concerned people who derived their livelihood from commercial and industrial occupations. In most cases the informants were males. It was found that divorces and separations were 6% and deaths of husbands or wives 10%. The scholar's findings were that 47% was positive, 42% neutral and 11% negative. By positive he means very successful marriages. By neutral he means a fair degree of harmony in domestic lives. And by negative he means disharmonious family lives. His conclusion is that these figures prove the efficacy of astrology in marital settlements.

The interrelations between the planetary and stellar positions and the sentiments of men and women are very intimate. Apart from the other astrological considerations, mutual dispositions of Mars and Venus are to be carefully considered. It cannot be a coincidence that divorce, separation and crimes of passion increase whenever there is a conjunction of Venus and Mars in the heavens, especially when the constellations involved are those of malefic planets. The Venus–Mars configuartion could of course be one of the contributing factors. Children born when there is a Venus–Mars conjunction should be brought up in a disciplined manner and should be made to avoid dissipating habits of immediate pleasure. The adverse effects of the conjunction could be made to express through constructive channels if Jupiter aspects the combination or is or is in a quadrant therefrom.

Venus is indeed associated with many fascinating aspects of life. He rules the wife, conveyance, sex harmony and union, art, attachment, family happiness, marriage in general, vitality, fertility, physical beauty and friendliness.

Mars abounds in energy, aggressiveness, fortitude, driving force and in association with Venus, a tendency to excess of sensual gratification.

It is therefore necessary that in the horoscopes of the couple, Mars–Venus conjunction or opposition should have a benefic steadying effect of a favourable disposition of Jupiter; or in the alternative the conjunction or opposition takes place in the constellations of Jupiter, Mercury or even Venus; Jupiter and Mercury being more preferable.

Venus-Mars disposition is an important factor for physical attraction. But in the absence of Jupiter's or even Saturn's benign influence, real compatibility may be lacking. Venus-Mars conjunction makes one fond of pleasure, demonstrative and adds zest to one's sensual life. When Venus and Mars are involved in adverse aspects, difficulty through excesses and trouble through marriage follow as a matter of consequence. Venus in a good sign or constellation can temper the roughness of Mars, but if Rahu is also involved, it makes one lascivious, lewed and wicked. Whether in the horoscope of a boy or a girl, Ketu-Venus-Mars association (or even mutual aspect) is not desirable unless the constellation involved belongs to Jupiter or Mercury or even benefic Moon, though the last circumstance might render the native's thinking highly sensual. Ketu-Venus-Mars (or Saturn) denotes danger of scandal in marriage. But if the 10th or house of Karma is well disposed, the affliction becomes somewhat tempered.

Let us take the example of a person having Venus-Mars conjunction in Taurus, the Lagna being Scorpio. Venus, Kalatrakaraka in the 7th, is not generally favoured by ancient writers on the theory of *karakobhavanasaya* as the indications of the 7th house are said to be inhibited. Experience has however revealed that this textual dictum is not quite valid. In fact Venus in the 7th is one of the finest combinations for a fairly happy marriage, denoting affection and attachment between the couple. When in the case under reference, Venus is in Krittika ruled by the Sun and Mars in Mrigasira, the 7th house gains considerable strength and the married life will be happy though crossed by frequent emotional clashes. If such a native is married to one who has Taurus rising with Venus and Mars in Scorpio, each will constantly try to appease the dictates of others' emotions and over-indulge in sensual pleasures to the detriment of their health. Venus in Taurus is good, but in a fiery constellation (Krittika) it gives rise to stubborness. In Rohini, on the other hand, the finer qualities of Venus find expression. It is always better to look for trinal or quadrangular dispositions of Mars and Venus from the Lagna or the Moon, no matter even if they conjoin provided they are in different constellations. A similar disposition in the partner's horoscope is desirable though not essential.

Just for illustration we give below a chart which is typical of a broken marriage. The native being a Hindu there was no legal divorce.

Sun	Moon Mercury		Sat.	Jupit.	Merc.		Ketu
Ketu Venus	RASI					NAVAMSA	Mars
			Rahu Mars	Sun			
				Sat. Venus			
	Ascdt. Mandi	Jupit.			Rahu	Ascdt.	Moon

Lord of the 7th Mars is in the 11th in combination with Rahu both in the constellations of Venus and aspected by Saturn posited in the constellation of Aridra. Venus, Kalatrakaraka in his turn, is much afflicted by association with Ketu, situated in the constellation of Rahu and aspected by Mars. Both the lord of the 7th and Venus have been much afflicted. The native married the daughter of a highly placed and respected officer. Before marriage, the girl's father had been advised to reject the boy as the girl's married life would not only suffer from untold misery, as the native could become a debauchee but she could be even rejected. The marriage took place. And to the amazement of the wife, she found that her husband was leading a profligate life and never loved her. All her attempts to wean him away from his evil ways failed, and from sheer disgust, the lady returned to her parent's house. The sensual life led by the native resulted in his contacting dreadful venereal complaints.

One cannot decide the make-up of a person—boy or girl—merely on the basis of the Moon's situation, though one can glean a few psychological facts. It is the total assessment of each horoscope that is to be considered before applying the tests for mutual compatibility.

In a number of charts of husbands and wives we have studied, the following peculiarities have been noticed.

When Venus, Mars and Jupiter in one horoscope are situated in the other horoscope in a trine or in an angle of 3 and 11 positions, that is, if in the husband's horoscope, Venus is in Taurus and in the wife's horoscope, in Cancer or Virgo or Scorpio, it is a favourable position. When the Sun and the Moon have similar harmonious positions, except 2 and 12 (*dwirdwadasa*), there is usually a strong attachment. Here again if the husband's Sun is in Cancer and the wife's in Virgo, the needed harmony exists. When the Sun and the Moon are disposed as suggested above but Mars in one case is in a sign which happens to be the 12th from Venus in the other horoscope, attachment exists, but there cannot be normal happiness in their private lives. If Venus in one horoscope is in a sign occupied by Saturn in the other a serious and industrious partner is indicated. Mars in the 7th, unaspected by benefics, indicates frequent quarrels leading to misunderstandings. Saturn in the 8th, aspected by Mars (especially 4th or 8th house aspect), is not conducive to mutual understanding. Saturn in the 7th confers stability in the marriage but the husband or wife manifests coldness and not warmth. A strong malefic in the 4th affects married happiness unless neutralised by a benefic aspect. If the Janma Rasi of the wife (or husband) happens to be the Lagna of the husband (or wife), or if the Lagna of the wife (or husband) happens to be the 7th (in the Horoscope) from the position of the lord or the 7th (in the other) the married life will be stable and built on mutual understanding and affection.

When certain afflictions are present in one horoscope it is said that they could be mitigated by having the native married to a partner whose horoscope has similar afflictions.

After satisfying on the basis of the birth horoscopes about the bride's (or bridegroom's) character, health, general mental soundness, the agreement between the two horoscopes is to be judged.

When evil combinations indicating misery in married life are present in the horoscope of a bride, then the same can be mitigated by marrying her to a boy whose horoscope has similar evil combinations. The evils can also be avoided by testing the marriage adaptability and by performing the marriages in proper Muhurthas.

Therefore with a view to avoid such unpleasant consequences, the astrological works of the Maharshis have laid down certain units of strength and agreement and when these are agreeable, the married couple would live happily in spite of external and physical discomforts like poverty, etc.

The Maharshis have claimed that by electing a proper time or Muhurtha for marriage, several of the evil indications in the charts of the couple can be minimised to a great extent.

In this chapter, I have confined myself to the elucidation of rules governing marriage adaptability. It is presumed that before applying these rules, the horoscopes have been judged already in regard to the 7th and 8th houses.

There are 12 factors to be considered in order to judge the suitability for a proposed matrimonial alliance out of which eight are supremely important. They are: (1) Dina, (2) Gana, (3) Mahendra, (4) Stree-Deergha, (5) Yoni, (6) Rasi, (7) Rasyadhipathi, (8) Vasya, (9) Rajju, (10) Vedha, (11) Varna, and (12) Nadi.

In order to illustrate these principles, we shall consider the horoscopes of a male and a female born in Mrigasira and Satabhisha respectively. It is assumed that the 7th and 8th houses are not only strong but are mutually well disposed.

1. **Dina Kuta.**—Count the constellation of the boy from that of the girl and divide the number by 9. If the remainder is 2, 4, 6, 8 or 0 it is good. The number of units of compatibility assigned to this Kuta is 3 in case agreement is found.

Example :—The constellation of the boy (*viz.*, Mrigasira in Taurus) counted from that of the girl (Dhanishta in Makara) gives 10. This divided by 9 leaves a remainder of 1 and hence there is no agreement, and no units of strength are scored on this account.

2. **Gana Kuta.**—This seems to have an important bearing on the temperament and character of the couple concerned. Compatibility of temperament and not of course identity of temperament is called for in astrology. A difference of temperament may be harmonious and complimentary. But a compatibility of temperament is essential to a satisfactory marriage union. Astrologically three Ganas (temperaments of natures) are recognised, viz., *Deva* (divine), *Manusha* (human), and *Rakshasa* (diabolical). Deva represents piety, goodness of character and charitable nature. Manusha is a mixture of good and bad, while Rakshasa suggests dominance, self-will and violence. These different natures are indicated by the birth constellation. A distaste for piety and religious disposition cannot be easily associated with piety and religious nature. A difference in beliefs and dogmas cannot always be overbalanced by sexual compatibility. Hence one born in a Deva constellation is not able to get on well with a person born in Rakshasa constellation. A *Deva* can marry a *Deva*, a *Manusha* can marry a *Manusha* and a *Rakshasa* can marry a *Rakshasa*.

Manusha or a Deva man should not marry a Rakshasa girl unless there are other neutralising factors. But marriage between a Rakshasa man and a Deva or Manusha girl is *passable*. If marriage is brought about between prohibited *Ganas* there will be quarrels and disharmony. So that the couple would always welcome an opportunity for separation and divorce. The following constellations denote the different Ganas :—

Deva Gana.—Punarvasu, Pushyami, Swati, Hasta, Sravana, Revati, Anuradha, Mrigasira and Aswini.

Manusha Gana.—Rohini, Pubba, Poorvashadha, Poorvabhadra, Bharani, Aridra, Uttara, Uttarashadha and Uttarabhadra.

Rakshasa Gana.—Krittika, Aslesha, Makha, Chitta, Visakha, Jyeshta, Moola, Dhanishta and Satabhisha.

The number of benefic units for agreement is 6.

Example :—Mrigasira comes under Deva Gana while Dhanishta comes under Rakshasa. Hence, Gana Kuta is absent.

If the asterism of the bride is beyond the 14th from that of the bridegroom the evil may be ignored.

3. **Mahendra.**—The constellation of the boy counted from that of the girl should be the 4th, 7th, 10th, 13th, 16th, 19th, 22nd or 25th. This promotes well-being and increases longevity.

Example :—Mrigasira (constellation of the boy) is the 10th from Dhanishta (girl's constellation). Hence good.

4. **Stree-Deergha.**—The boy's constellation should preferably be beyond the 9th from that of the girl. According to some authorities the distance should be more than 7 constellations.

Exception : This consideration may be ignored if *Rasi Kuta* and *Graha Maitri* obtain.

Example :—Mrigasira is *beyond* 9 constellations from Dhanishta. Hence agreement in regard to Stree-Deergha is present.

5. **Yoni Kuta.**—Yoni means sex and by Yoni Kuta is implied sexual compatibility. The sexual urge of a person born for instance in Chitta is supposed to be as strong as that of a tiger. The human embryo in course of its development passes through the various stages of evolution—mammals, quadrupeds, etc., so that the tendencies of certain animals will be predominant. The birth constellation seems to show this predominance.

Each sign and degree of the zodiac expresses the degree of evolution of the individual concerned. Thus, one born in Leo will have in him the characteristics of a lion while the other born in Aries will be timid and mild. It is these biological influences that seem to be at the root of all astrological considerations. If both the couple belong to the male constellations, there will be frequent quarrels and want of agreement in sex-matters. So the best way is to mate a male belonging to a male constellation with a female belonging to a female constellation. The Kutas in general lay down the foundation for marriage happiness.

Therefore the Yoni Kuta takes into account the sexual aspect of marriage and indicates the sex affinities such as the degree of sex-urge, sex-compatibility, the size of copulatory organs and so on. Havelock Ellis says that "out of 500 consecutive cases coming for advice (1930) all but one showed sexual maladjustment as a complicating factor". This reveals to us the importance of Yoni Kuta. All the 27 constellations have been assigned certain animals and sexes as given below :—

	Male	Female	Class of Yoni
1	Aswini	Satabhisha	Horse
2	Bharani	Revati	Elephant
3	Pushya	Krittika	Sheep
4	Rohini	Mrigasira	Serpent
5	Moola	Aridra	Dog
6	Aslesha	Punarvasu	Cat
7	Makha	Pubba	Rat
8	Uttara	Uttarabhadra	Cow
9	Swati	Hasta	Buffalo
10	Visakha	Chitta	Tiger
11	Jyeshta	Anuradha	Hare
12	Poorvashadha	Sravana	Monkey
13	Poorvabhadra	Danishta	Lion
14	Uttarashadha		Mongoose

Marriage

Marriage between the constellations indicating same class of yoni and between the male and female stars of that yoni said to conduce to great happiness, perfect harmony and progeny. If the male and female happen to be born in friendly yonis, but both representing female constellations there will be fair happiness and agreement. If the couple belong both to male constellations there will be constant quarrels and unhappiness. If marriage takes place between constellations indicating unfriendly yonis it is better marriage is avoided. For example, if marriage takes place between a male born in Moola and female born in Aridra it will turn out a very happy. The constellations Moola and Aridra represent the male and female organs of a dog. The union of these is agreeable and conduces to favourable results to the fullest extent. If marriage takes place between a man born in the constellation Satabhisha and a girl born in Punarvasu, both representing the female stars, the marriage is passable but not so good as in the first instance. Marriages between persons belonging to constellations indicating inimical yonis are not recommended. The number of units for **Yoni Kuta** is 4.

Example :—Both Mrigasira and Dhanishta are female constellations, the one typifying the yoni of a serpent and the other that of a lion. Hence, Yoni Kuta is not present.

The following pairs are hostile and in matching Yoni Kuta, they should be avoided :—

Cow and tiger; elephant and lion; horse and buffalo; dog and hare; serpent and mongoose; monkey and goat; and cat and rat. In a similar way, similar pairs of constellations typifying other hostile pairs as they occur in nature should be avoided (see Table on page 72).

In the following table, units for matching different Yonis are given. Suppose the boy's star is Krittika signifying the Yoni of sheep and the girl's star is Chitta signifying tiger. In the column "sheep" running down our eye in the horizontal column against tiger, the unit of agreements is I.

Yoni	Horse	Elephant	Sheep	Serpent	Dog	Cat	Rat	Cow	Buffalo	Tiger	Hare	Monkey	Mongoose	Lion
Horse	4	2	2	3	2	2	2	1	0	1	3	3	2	1
Elephant	2	4	3	3	2	2	2	2	3	1	2	3	2	0
Sheep	2	3	4	2	1	2	1	3	3	1	2	0	3	1
Serpent	3	3	2	4	2	1	1	1	1	1	2	2	0	2
Dog	2	2	1	2	4	2	1	2	2	1	0	2	1	1
Cat	2	2	2	1	2	4	0	2	2	2	3	3	2	2
Rat	2	2	1	1	1	0	4	2	2	1	2	2	1	1
Cow	1	2	3	1	2	2	2	4	3	0	3	2	2	2
Buffalo	0	3	3	1	2	2	2	3	4	1	2	1	2	1
Tiger	1	1	1	2	1	1	2	0	1	4	1	1	2	1
Hare	3	2	2	2	0	3	2	3	2	1	4	2	2	1
Monkey	3	3	0	2	2	3	2	2	2	1	2	4	3	2
Mongoose	2	2	3	0	1	2	1	2	2	2	2	3	4	2
Lion	1	0	1	2	1	1	2	1	2	1	1	2	2	4

6. Rasi Kuta.—If the Rasi of the boy happens to be the 2nd from that of the girl and if the Rasi of the girl happens to be the 12th from that of the boy, evil results will follow. But if, on the other hand, the Rasi of the boy falls in the 12th from the girl's or the Rasi of the girl is in the 2nd from that of the boy astrology predicts longevity for the couple. If the Rasi of the boy is the 3rd from that of the girl, there will be misery and sorrow. But if the Rasi of the girl is the 3rd from that of the boy, there will be happiness. If the boy's falls in the 4th from that of the girl's, then there will be great poverty; but if the Rasi of the girl happens to fall in the 4th from the boy's there will be great wealth. If the boy's Rasi falls in the 5th from that of the girl, there will be unhappiness. But if the girl's Rasi falls in the 5th from that of the boy, there will be enjoyment and prosperity. But where the Rasis of the boy and the girl are in the 7th houses mutually, then there will be health, agreement and happiness. If the boy's Rasi falls in the 6th from the girl's there will be loss of children, but if the girl's is the 6th from the boy's, then the progeny will prosper.

The number of units for **Rasi Kuta is 7.**

Exception :— When both the Rasis are owned by one planet or if the lords of the two Rasis happen to be friends, the evil attributed above to the inauspicious disposition of Rasis gets cancelled.

7. Rasyadhipathi or Graha Maitram.—This is the most important Kuta inasmuch as it deals with the psychological dispositions of the couple. The mental qualities of the parties and their affection for each other are admittedly of vital importance to their happiness. This must be tested before marriage. In considering *Graha Maitram* the friendship or otherwise between the lords of the Janma Rasis of the persons concerned is very important. Planetary friendships are given in almost all astrological works. But still I give below a table indicating the relations between the different planets so that the reader may not have to refer to other books.

Planetary Friendships

	Friend	Neutral	Enemy
The Sun	Moon, Mars, Jupiter	Mercury	Saturn Venus
The Moon	Sun, Mercury	Mars, Jupiter Venus, Saturn	
Mars	Sun, Moon, Jupiter	Venus, Saturn	Merc.
Mercury	Sun, Venus	Mars, Jupiter, Saturn	Moon
Jupiter	Sun, Moon, Mars	Saturn	Merc., Venus
Venus	Mercury, Saturn	Mars, Jupiter	Sun, Moon
Saturn	Mercury, Venus	Jupiter	Sun, Moon, Mars

Some suggest that in considering the planetary relations, the temporary dispositions should also be taken into account. This in my humble opinion is not necessary, because, the entire subject of adaptability hinges on the birth constellations and not on birth charts as a whole.

When the lords of the Janma Rasis of the bride and bridegroom are friends, the Rasi Kuta is said to obtain in full. When one is a friend and the other is a neutral, it is passable. When both are neutral, Rasi Kuta is very ordinary. When both are enemies, Rasi Kuta does not exist.

Exception :—Even when there is no friendship between the Janma Rasi lords of the bridegroom and bride, Rasi Kuta may be said to exist if friendship prevails between the planets owning the Navamsas occupied by the Moon.

The number of units for this **Kuta is 5.**

Example :— In our illustration, the Janma Rasi lords are Venus and Saturn. Both are friends. Therefore Rasi Kuta is complete. Supposing the bride and bridegroom are born in Makha 2 (Leo) and Satabhisha 2 (Saturn). The lords will be the Sun and Saturn respectively and they are not friends. In such a case if the Navamsa relationship is considered, then the Moon will be in Taurus (Venus) and Capricorn (Saturn) respectively. Venus and Saturn are friends and therefore the match is permissible. One will have to be very careful in the assessment of these factors and on superficial grounds no horoscope should be rejected as unsuitable or unfortunate.

8. **Vasya Kuta.**—This is important as suggesting the degree of magnetic control or amenability the wife or husband would be able to exercise on the other. For Aries—Leo and Scorpio are amenable. For Taurus—Cancer and Libra ; for Gemini—Virgo; for Cancer—Scorpo and Sagittarius ; for Leo—Libra ; for Virgo—Pisces and Gemini ; for Libra—Capricorn and Virgo ; for Scorpio—Cancer ; for Sagittarius—Pisces ; for Capricorn—Aries and Aquarius ; for Aquarius—Aries ; and for Pisces—Capricorn. The unit of agreement is **2.**

Example :—In our illustration, neither the boy's nor the girl's horoscope is subject to the control of the other.

9. **Rajju.**—This indicates the strength or duration of married life and therefore it merits special attention.

The 27 constellations have been grouped into five types of Rajju.

Padarajju.—Aswini, Aslesha, Makha, Jyeshta, Moola, Revati.

Katirajju.—Bharani, Pushyami, Pubba, Anuradha, Poorvashadha, Uttarabhadra.

Nabhi or Udararajju.—Krittika, Punarvasu, Uttara, Visakha, Uttarashadha, Poorvabhadra.

Kantarajju.—Rohini, Aridra Hasta, Swati, Sravana, and Satabhisha.

Sirorajju.—Dhanishta, Chitta and Mrigasira.

The Janma Nakshatras of the couple should not fall in the same rajju. If they fall in Sira (head) husband's death is likely; if in Kantha (neck) the wife may die; if in Udara (stomach) the children may die; if in Kati (waist) poverty may ensue; and if in Pada (foot) the couple may be always wandering. Hence, it is desirable that the boy and the girl have constellations belonging to different rajjus or groups.

10 Vedha.—This means affliction. Certain constellations are capable of affecting or afflicting certain other constellations situated at particular distances from them. For instance, Aswini is said to cause Vedha to 18th constellation (*viz.*, Jyeshta) from it; Bharani to the 16th (*viz.*, Anuradha) and so on. The following pairs of constellations affect each other and, therefore, no marriage should be brought about between a boy and girl whose Janma Nakshatras belong to the same pair unless there are other relieving factors.

Aswini and Jyeshta; Bharani and Anuradha; Krittika and Visakha; Rohini and Swati; Aridra and Sravana, Punarvasu and Uttarashadha; Pusayami and Poorvashadha; Aslesha and Moola; Makha and Revati; Pubba and Uttarabhadra; Uttara and Poorvabhadra; Hasta and

Satabhisha, Mrigasira and Dhanishta. In our example, the constellations of the couple (Mrigasira and Dhanishta) belong to the prohibited pair and hence Vedhakuta is absent.

11. Varna.—This seems to signify the degree of spiritual or ego development of the marrying partners. Pisces, Scorpio and Cancer represent the highest development—Brahmin; Leo, Sagittarius and Libra indicate the second grade—or Kshatriya; Aries, Gemini and Aquarius suggest the third or the Vaisya; while Taurus, Virgo and Capricorn indicate the last grade, *viz.*, Sudra. A girl belonging to a higher grade of spiritual development should not be mated to a boy of lesser development. The *vice versa* or both belonging to the same grade or degree is allowed.

The unit of agreement is 1

12. Nadi Kuta.—This is considered to be the most important and at the same time the most significant Kuta. In Sanskrit, Nadi means several things but in reference to astrology, it signifies pulse or nervous energy indicating the physiological and to a certain extent hereditary factors. The Hindu medical works enumerate three *Nadis* or humours, *viz.*, *Vatha* (wind), *Pitha* (bile) and *Sleshma* (phlegm). A boy with a predominantly windy or phlegmatic or bilious constitution should not marry a girl of the same type. The girl should belong to a different temperament. The three Nadis are ruled by the different constellations as follows:—

Vata	*Pitha*	*Sleshma*
Aswini	Bharani	Krittika
Aridra	Mrigasira	Rohini
Punarvasu	Pushyami	Aslesha
Uttara	Pubba	Makha

Vata	Pitha	Sleshma
Hasta	Chitta	Swati
Jyeshta	Anuradha	Visakha
Moola	Poorvashadha	Uttarashadha
Satabhisha	Dhanishta	Sravana
Poorvabhadra	Uttarabhadra	Revati

If the constellation of the boy and girl fall in different rows, then agreement between the couple will be good. They should not fall in the middle. Stars of the couple may fall in the first and the last line *under certain* circumstances.

If Nadi Kuta is not present on the basis of the Nakshatras, then the same may be reckoned taking into account the *Nakshatra Padas*. Thus, the different quarters will be governed by the three humours (Nadis) thus:

Aswini 1	Aswini 2	Aswini 3
Bharani 2	Bharani 1	Aswini 4
Bharani 3	Bharani 4	Krittika 1
Krittika 4	Krittika 3	Krittika 2
Rohini 1	Rohini 2	Rohini 3

Beginning from Aswini 1, the counting should be done forwards and backwards in threes as given above.

The unit ascribed for this Kuta is 8.

In the example considered above, both the constellations fall in the middle line and hence Nadi Kuta is completely absent.

Appendix 1 gives a table for measuring the agreement units. In the first column (longitudinal) the constellations of the bride are given.

In the first horizontal column, the boy's nakshatra is given. Take the figure in the column where the girl's and the boy's stars interesect. Suppose the boy's star is Mrigasira 1, the Rasi being Taurus.

The girl's star is Satabhisha 2, Rasi being Kumbha. Running down our eye from Taurus, Mrigasira 2 (horizontal first column) to the horizontal line of Satabhisha 4, Kumbha, we find the figure 26.5 as the total units of agreement.

Special Considerations

We have dealt with above, fairly exhaustively, the question of marriage adaptability and the importance of the various *Kutas* or physiological and psychological junctions in the human body and how a consideration of each Kuta would enable us to appreciate the harmony or discord likely to prevail between intending marriage partners.

Exceptions

We shall now give certain contingencies arising by virtue of common Janma Rasi, common birth star and the absence of certain Kutas.

(1) The absence of Stree-Deerga may be ignored if Rasi Kuta add Graha Maitri are present.

(2) If the Rasi of the girl is odd, the 6th and 8th Rasis therefrom are friendly. If the Rasi of the girl is even the 2nd and 12th therefrom become friendly. The evil due to the birth of the bride in a Rakshasa gana star may be ignored if Janma Rasi being 2nd and 12th, 9th and 5th or 6th and 8th, the lords of the Rasis are the same or are mutual friends.

(3) Though Graha Maitri is by far the most important, it need not be considered if the couple have their Janma Rasis disposed in one and seven from each other.

(4) Rajju Kuta need not be considered in case Graha Maitri, Rasi, Dina and Mahendra Kutas are present.

(5) The evil due to Nadi Kuta can be ignored subject to the following conditions :—

(a) The Rasi and Rajju Kuta prevail. (b) The same planet is lord of the Janma Rasis of both the male and the female. (c) The lords of the Janma Rasis of the couple are friends.

In many cases, the Janma Rasis of the Janma Nakshatras of the bride and bridegroom would be the same. Special attention is paid by astrological writers to such exceptions and we shall throw some light on them for the edification of our readers.

Common Janma Rasi.— Views differ as regards the results accruing from the Janma Rasis being common. According to Narada, common Janma Rasi would be conducive to the couple provided they are born in different constellations. Garga opines that under the above circumstance, the asterism of the boy should precede that of the girl if the marriage is to prove happy. In case the reverse holds good (Stree-purva), *i e.*, the constellation of the girl precedes that of the boy, the alliance should be rejected. This view is supported by other sages, *viz.*, Brihaspathi and Bhrigu. In fact, the author of *Muhurtha Thathwa* goes to the extent of saying that in cases of common Janma Rasi, provided the man's constellation is preceding the girl's, the Kutas or adaptability need not be applied at all.

Common Janma Nakshatra.—This is a further extension of the principle of common Janma Rasi. The Janma Nakshatras of the bride and bridegroom, being one and the same, are approved in case of Rohini, Aridra, Makha, Hasta, Visakha, Sravana, Uttarabhadra and Revati. The effect would be ordinary if the common Janma Nakshatras are Aswini, Krittika, Mrigasira, Punarvasu, Pushya, Pubba, Uttara, Chitta, Anuradha, Poorvashadha and

Uttarashadha, Bharani, Aslesha, Swati, Jyeshta, Moola, Dhanishta, Satabhisha and Poorvabhadra happening to be common Janma Nakshatras are not recommended.

Here again certain ancient authors hold that even though the Janma Nakshatras are same, the evil becomes nullified if the Padas are different. If the Janma Nakshatra belongs to two signs (*e.g.*, Krittika) the Pada of the bride should relate to the preceding sign. For example, if Krittika is the common Janma Nakshatra, the bride should have her Janma Rasi in Mesha and the bridegroom in Vrishabha. If, however, the common Janma Nakshatra belongs to two signs equally (*e.g.*, Mrigasira, Chitta, etc.) the sign for the first two quarters should be that of the bridegroom.

The couple should not have the same Janma Rasi, same Janma Nakshatra and Pada. However, in regard to Satabhisha, Hasta, Swati, Aswini, Krittika, Poorvashadha, Mrigasira and Makha, the evil given rise to by virtue of common Janma Rasi, Nakshatra and Pada gets cancelled if the couple are born in the first quarter.

Destructive Constellations

There is a belief current amongst the public that girls born in certain constellations cause the death of certain relatives. For instance, a girl born in Visakha is said to bring about the destruction of her husband's younger brother so that parents generally try to find out a bridegroom who does not have a younger brother. Even when there are other merits in the horoscope, it is rejected on the simple ground that the girl is born in Visakha. This is entirely due to ignorance of the real astrological factors governing such considerations. Only certain Padas or quarters should be held inauspicious and not the entire constellation. Thus, in regard to Visakha, only the last quarter is evil and not the first three. Therefore a girl born in the first three quarters of Visakha should not be considered to bring misfortune to her husband's youger brother. Similarly, the boy or girl born in the first quarter of Moola is to be rejected as it is said to cause the death of the father-in-law. The last three quarters of Moola are beneficial. A girl born in Jyeshta is said to cause evil to her husband's elder brother. Almost all authors agree that (certain parts of) Moola, Aslesha, Jyeshta and Visakha are destructive constellations—Moola (first quarter) for husband's father; Aslesha (first quarter) for husband's mother; Jyeshta (first quarter) for girl's husband's elder brother; and Visakha (last quarter) for husband's younger brother.*

The So-called Kuja Dosha

The position of Venus and Mars is very important in judging marital relations. Mars whose element is fire rules marriage. Where he is badly situated or associated in the horoscope of a male or female, it follows that the sacerdotal fire gets extinguished soon. Such unfavourable situation goes under the name of *Kuja Dosha*.

It must be noted that in determining marriage adaptability between two parties, there are several elements of much more importance than *Kuja Dosha*. And the evil influences accuring from the bad position of Mars is only one of the several elements.

It is unfortunate that throughout South India especially in the Tamil areas, much is made of the so-called *Kuja Dosham* and this bugbear has been the means of destroying the happiness of many families by preventing

---

* Mooladou swasuram hanti vyaladouca bhidhankanam
Jyeshtadou jyeshtajam hanti visakhantecha devaram

Marriage

marriages otherwise very eligible and anxiously wished for. So far as our humble experience goes it is only in the *Kerala Sastra* that mention is made of Kuja Dosha. The stanza runs thus : *Dhana vyayecha pathale jamitre chashtame kuja* ; *Strinam bharthru vinasamcha bharthunam strivinasanam.* This means :—"If Mars is in the 2nd, 12th, 4th, 7th and 8th houses in the horoscope of the female, the death of the husband will occur ; similar situation in the husband's horoscope causes the death of wife."

The Lagna represents body, the Moon, mind and Venus, sexual relations. Therefore, the houses have to be reckoned with reference to all the three, *viz.,* Lagna, Moon and Venus. The dosha (evil) is considered weak when it exists from Lagna, a little stronger from the Moon and still more powerful from Venus.

The second house signifies family ; the twelfth represents comforts and pleasures of bed. The fourth rules sukha or happiness. The seventh indicates husband and eighth represents longevity of the wife or husband. Hence the position of Mars in these houses is supposed to produce this peculiar dosham or evil. If Kuja Dosham obtains in the horoscopes of both the bride and bridegroom, the dosham gets cancelled. There are, of course, many good combinations which assure marital felicity and much importance need not be given to Kuja Dosham.

Granting that Kuja Dosham is a factor whose occurrence should not be ignored, there are antidotes which are not generally known to the rank and file of Hindu astrologers. The exceptions are : Mars in the 2nd can be said to be bad provided such 2nd house is any other than Gemini and Virgo ; in the 12th the dosha is produced when such 12th house is any other than Taurus and Libra ; in the 4th house Mars causes dosha provided the house falls in any sign other than Aries and Scorpio; when the 7th is other than Capricorn and Cancer, the dosha is given rise to; and Mars gives bad effects in the 8th, provided the 8th is any other than Sagittarius and Pisces. In Aquarius and Leo, Mars produces no dosha whatsoever. The dosha is counteracted by the conjunction of Mars and Jupiter or Mars and the Moon; or by the presence of Jupiter or Venus in the ascendant.

Thus, it will be seen that Kuja Dosha does not deserve that consideration which is now being paid to it. In the consideration of marriage adaptability there are various other factors which should be carefully examined.

We have dealt above fairly exhaustively with the question of marriage adaptability and have tried to avoid controversial issues as the book is intended for the common man who wishes to take advantage of the astrological rules to his benefit.

Electing a Time for Marriage

Ordinarily almost every Indian Panchanga gives important dates and times for celebrating marriages. The reader cannot rely on them as most of the dates given would not be free from important flaws. Moreover, the marriage dates selected would generally be in accordance with local usages. For instance, a Tamilian would not mind marriage being performed in lunar month of Ashadha (provided the Sun has not entered Cancer). But strong objection is taken to this by people living in Andhra and Karnataka. Apart from this, there is universal agreement all over India as regards the time, weekday, constellation and planetary positions to be obtained at the time of marriage.

I am giving below the most standard methods employed by scholars, warranted by experience and sanctioned by the ancient sages.

The lunar months of Magha, Phalguna, Vaisakha and Jyeshta are good. Kartika and Margasira are ordinary. The rest are not auspicious. Some sages opine that marriages can be celebrated in Pushya and Chaitra provided the Sun is in Capricorn and Aries respectively.

The following lunar days, *viz.*, from the 11th day (dark half) to New Moon, Riktha Thithis, 8th, 12th and 6th should be rejected. The best lunar days are the 2nd, 3rd, 5th, 7th, 10th, 11th and 13th (of the bright half).

Monday, Wednesday, Thursday and Friday are the best. Sunday and Saturday are middling. And Tuesday should be invariably rejected.

The best asterisms are Rohini, Mrigasira, Makha, Uttara, Hasta, Swati, Anuradha, Moola, Uttarashadha, Uttarabhadra and Revati. The first quarter of Makha and Moola and the last quarter of Revati are inauspicious and they should be rejected. Constellations not mentioned here are unsuitable and they should be avoided.

The following yogas should be rejected: Vyatipata, Dhruva, Mrityu, Ganda, Vajra, Soola, Vishkambha, Atiganda, Vyaghata and Parigha.

Vishtikarana must invariably be discarded.

Among the zodiacal signs Gemini, Virgo and Libra are the best. Taurus, Cancer, Leo, Sagittarius and Aquarius are middling. The rest are inauspicious.

In the election of a Muhurtha for marriage, as many of the 21 doshas (already mentioned) as possible should be avoided. The most important considerations however are (*a*) The 7th house must be unoccupied by any planet, (*b*) Mars should not be in the 8th, (*c*) Venus should not be in the 6th, (d) the Lagna should not be hemmed in between malefics, (e) malefics should not occupy Lagna, and (f) the Moon in the election chart should have no association with any other planet.

Apart from the above, the usual Tarabala, Panchaka, etc., should be looked into. Elsewhere are given certain special combinations which are supposed to neutralise adverse influeces. As far as possible, such combinations should be applied to secure a really propitious moment. Jupiter, Mercury or Venus in Lagna, malefics in the 3rd or 11th, would constitute a formidable force in rendering the Lagna strong. The following are some of the special combinations which are supposed to fortify the marriage election chart :—

(1) Jupiter in the ascendant, Venus in the 8th and the Sun in the 11th—Mahendra Yoga.

(2) Venus in Lagna, Jupiter in the 10th and the Sun and Mercury in the 11th—Vishnu Priya Yoga.

(3) Venus in the 2nd, Jupiter in the 12th, the Sun in the 8th and Saturn in the 6th—Sreenatha Yoga.

(4) Venus in Lagna, Jupiter in the 4th, Mercury in the 2nd and Saturn in the 11th—Samudra Yoga.

(5) Mercury, Jupiter and Venus in Lagna—Vijaya Yoga.

(6) Venus and Jupiter in Lagna elevated or otherwise strong—Jaya Yoga.

(7) Saturn in the 3rd, Jupiter in the 6th, the Sun in the 10th and Mars in the 11th—Pushya Yoga.

(8) Mars in the 3rd, Saturn in the 6th, Venus in the 9th, Jupiter in the 12th—Maharshi Yoga.

(9) Venus in Lagna, Jupiter in the 11th—Ardhama Yoga.

Thus, it will be seen that the Hindus have devised an astrological means of judging marriage compatibility whereby the relations between the couple may stand the strain of maladjustment. If astrological advices are properly heeded to, there will be fewer tragedies than at present and less marital infidelity. Modern sexologists and sociologists will do well to study the theory behind the astrological rules bearing on marriage casting off their prejudices instead of criticising and condemning the system.

CHAPTER X

Elections Concerning General Matters

In this chapter, I propose to deal with such elections as have a bearing on the personal life of an individual. For instance, one has to buy or sell shares, buy or wear new clothes, etc. Auspicious times could be fixed for all such important daily activities.

Wearing New Clothes.—Aswini, Rohini, Punarvasu, Pushyami, Uttara, Hasta, Chitta, Swati, Visakha, Dhanishta and Revati are the best. Monday, Wednesday, Thursday and Friday are good. Sunday is middling. Tuesday and Saturday are inauspicious. The 4th, 9th, 14th lunar days and New Moon day should be avoided. The Moon should be as far as possible in good aspect to the Sun.

Forming a Library.—Mercury should be in exaltation or occupy the Lagna. Thursday is the best. Fortify Lagna by placing a malefic in the 11th.

Employing Servants.—Avoid Tuesdays and Saturdays. Look to the strength of the 11th house lord. Saturn must be in the 11th free from the aspect of Mars or Rahu.

Make the lord of the sixth occupy the 11th and as far as possible, choose a fixed sign. Afflictions to Mercury should also be avoided as they bring about theft in the house.

Shaving.—There are certain people who seem to be under the delusion that the ancients were a set of fools and that their observations of phenomena—in their various aspects—do not merit the attention of the modern man. Many of the modern scientific discoveries had been anticipated by the ancients. Possessing a splendid language which stands unrivalled even to this day in its powers of expression and brevity, they employed Sanskrit words which embodied their scientific discoveries unmistakably. Intellectual prejudices go a great deal to warp the judgement of even the greatest men and some so-called men of science have entirely fallen into this inviting snare. The hair-splitting philosophers of the East, says the intellectual upstart of the modern day, do not deserve the slightest consideration for their scientific knowledge. The means by which the ancient Maharshis pursued their intellectual studies are not well known to us, but the fragments of literary and scientific works left to us by the Rishis have their own intrinsic value.

In the article entitled "Moon and Terrestrial Life", published in the April 1943 issue of *The Astrological Magazine*, Mr. M. V. Ramakrishnan has shown the periodicity existing between certain happenings on terrestrial life and the lunar movements. The following sentences which I am extracting from the article in question are significant. "Persons who wish their hair to grow dense and long should cut it in the first half of the Moon. Nails should be cut at the waxing period to give them a good chance of growing." Compare this with the principles given in Muhurtha works especially regarding the injunctions pertaining to shaving. People seem to laugh at the idea when astrologers tell them that they should have this operation on particular days at particular times

The science of electricity was known to the ancients and it was the late Prof. B. Suryanarain Rao that was responsible for bringing into light this important fact. The human body is a bundle of electrical currents and the hairs and nails are channels through which this electricity is discharged. With a view to concentrate and preserve all good energies in man and to dissipate and get rid of all evil forces in the human body, the Maharshis have laid down certain rules, which when studied by themselves look quite arbitrary and meaningless, but which when carefully examined in the light of conservation of energy-principle look most wonderful and striking with regard to the knowledge possessed by them in physical sciences.

According to Maharshi Vatsyayana, *akshi* (eyes), *vaksha* (chest), *kukshi* (stomach), *sira* (head), *hridi* (heart), *hastam* (hands), *apatsu* (feminine sexual organ), *nabhi* (navel), *medhra* (male sexual organ), *adhobhaga nalayuha* (lower intestines), *buddisthana* (seat of intelligence of brain) and *brahmadanda* (the seat of the ray of the Brahma) are all seats of electricity. Hence the cutting of hair from the head means so much loss of vitality of the body. On certain lunar days owing to the nature of the electrical energies coming from the Moon—such loss of vitality from the body can be neutralised. Hence the injunction that shaving should be had recourse to at such times as would minimise or neutralise the flow of electric currents from these sources.

If a man shaves after food, he commits a great blunder as the electrical currents from his body, which are about to be discharged by the digestion of food, are harmfully interfered with, and as a natural consequence his health may be affected in course of time. Shaving means cutting off hair from some part of the head and face and this again means loss of electricity which is so very essential for the proper upkeep of the physical and mental faculties of an individual.

People inclined towards the practice of spiritual precepts generally grow beards. The idea is to avoid waste of energy. Eye defects, loss of memory, loss of sight, deafness and other injurious consequences are directly traceable to promiscuous shaving without reference to day or time and many physical ills of man may be minimised by regulating "Shaving" in the light of astrological principles.

Shaving may be had in the constellation of Pushya, Punarvasu, Revati, Hasta, Sravana, Dhanishta, Mrigasira, Aswini, Chitta, Jyeshta, Satabhisha and Swati. 4th, 6th and 14th lunar days as also New Moon and Full Moon days are not desirable. Similar considerations have held good in the matter of death and birth pollution and solar and lunar eclipses. The ancients studied sciences and laid down strict injunctions so that humanity may be benefited. They did not believe in simply cataloguing facts as we in modern times do. These may be sour grapes for those who are blinded by thick prejudices but they are sweet for those who have a clear mental vision and who wish to economise the waste of spiritual energy for their own ultimate good.

Cutting Nails.—Avoid Fridays and Saturdays—the 8th, 9th, 14th lunar days as well as New and Full Moon days. Cutting nails means discharge of electricity from the human body and one should be careful to see that the reaction on the human body is not adverse.

Buying Utensils, etc.—Place Jupiter in good aspect to the Moon while buying brass vessels; to Mars when buying vessels of copper; to Saturn if steel and iron; to ascendant if of silver. Avoid the asterisms of Aslesha, Moola and Jyeshta. For buying tools, similarly avoid the 8th and 9th lunar days and New Moon.

Buying Jewellery.—The Sun and the Moon should be well situated and aspected. As usual unfavourable lunar days and asterisms should be avoided.

Lending Money.—One should not lend money on days ruled by Krittika, Makha, Moola, Satabhisha, Uttara, Punarvasu or one's Janma Nakshatra day. One should try to receive money on these days. Tuesdays and Fridays are also inauspicious. Never lend money on a New Moon day happening to be Saturday. The lords of the ascendant and the 7th should be harmoniously disposed. The Moon's situation in Scorpio is bad for the lender.

Borrowing Money.—Do not borrow money on days ruled by Krittika, Moola, Punarvasu, Dhanishta and Janma Nakshatra. Moon's conjunction with Mars and Saturn should be avoided as otherwise there will be quarrels and litigation. If the money is intended for quick use on domestic or personal matters, the Moon should be in good aspect to the ascendant. If the borrowed money is to be spent on business, the Moon must be in a favourable situation with regard to Mercury and lord of Lagna. For any election, purity of lunar day, weekday, any constellation and Tarabala are essential and further considerations come in only later on.

Buying for Business.—Thursday, the 10th lunar day and the constellation of Pushyami are the best. Tuesday should be completely rejected. Saturday is passable. Mercury, the 2nd lord and the 2nd house should all be fortified. Avoid buying for trade when Mercury is afflicted by Mars as this will destroy stocks and cause discord and wrangling. Mercury and Jupiter in conjunction in Lagna or in mutual aspects would be highly propitious.

Elections Concerning General Matters

Buying Cattle.—Monday, Tuesday, Wednesday and Saturday are good. The lord of the day in question should occupy the rising sign at the time of transaction. To *buy sheep* the propitoius time is that on a Thursday ruled by Pushya when Aries is rising.

Selling for Profit.—Let the Moon and Mercury be free from the conjunction or aspect of Mars. The Moon's situation in Taurus, Cancer or Pisces would greatly help the seller. Try to keep Mercury in a kendra from Lagna or at least in good aspect to Jupiter. Tuesday should be avoided. Monday, Wednesday and Thursday are the best. While Friday is unpropitious, Saturday is middling.

Shifting from Place to Place. More details are given in Chapter XIII. If one is to move *urgently* from one place to another, Janma Nakshatra should be avoided. Anuradha, Mrigasira and Hasta are the best. Journey on the 9th lunar day is prohibited. Yet in cases of urgency, one can move at a propitious moment. If you desire pecuniary gain conform to all the astrological requirements suggested in Chapter XIV. In any case, let there be Tarabala and Chandrabala and let the ascendant be fortified. The Moon and the ascendant should both be in fixed signs. Jupiter or Venus should be in an angle preferably in the ascendant or the 10th.

Recovering Money Due.—The lord of Lagna should be strong and the election rising sign should not fall in the 8th or 9th from the radical rising sign. The lords of Lagna and the 2nd must also be well situated.

Pledging.—Articles pledged under Visakha, Krittika (Sadhana), Bharani, Makha, Pubba, Poorvashadha, Poorvabhadra (Vajra), Aridra, Aslesha, Jyeshta and Moola (Theeshana) do not return. Jupiter and the Moon should be *mutually* well disposed. Tuesdays and Fridays are inauspicious as also lunar days declared generally evil.

Making a Will.—The Moon, the Lagna and the lord of the Lagna should all be in fixed signs. The constellation of Pushyami is the best as also Wednesday and Thursday. Tuesday and Friday should be avoided. For the benefit of the legatee, the rising sign should be one of Jupiter or Venus. Let Mars and Saturn be in the 3rd or 11th house. The 8th house must also be rendered strong as otherwise the testator will die.

CHAPTER XI

Elections Pertaining to Education

According to ancient sages *Vidya or Education* comprises the study of the Vedas, Vedangas, Mimamsa, Dharmasastras, Medicine, Music, Political Sciences and Economic subjects. Elaborate treatises exist on all these subjects. In order to get proficiency in the different branches of knowledge, education should be commenced under auspicious planetary influences. Each subject in which mastery is desired calls for concentration to be applied in a particular form with a view to tapping the intellectual resources of the particular type—latent in the brain cells. Astrological consultation is held to facilitate such concentration as the moment selected for commencing the study of a particular subject is supposed to tune the mental currents to be in harmony with the natural forces.

The most beneficial constellations for commencing education are Mrigasira, Aridra, Punarvasu, Pushya, Hasta, Chitta, Swati, Sravana, Dhanishta and Satabhisha. Aswini is held by some writers to be one of the best. Rohini, Uttara, Uttarashadha and Revati are neutral. The remaining ones are to be rejected.

Tuesday and Saturday should invariably be avoided. Sunday can be considered permissible if other astrological conditions are satisfactory. The following lunar days are auspicious:—1st (of dark half), 2nd, 3rd, 5th, 6th,

10th and 11th. The 4th, 8th, 9th, 14th and New and Full Moon days should be avoided.

The Lagna should not be a fixed sign. Common signs are the best and the movable ones ordinary.

In commencing education - be it of any type—one should have regard to two important Yogas given below :—

Saraswati Yoga—

(a) Wednesday coinciding with Hasta, the rising sign at the time being Gemini or Virgo with the Sun, Moon and Mercury occupying the Amsa of Mercury.

(b) Wednesday at sunrise when Mercury is in deep exaltation.

(c) Wednesday when Mercury is in Lagna and occupies the 3rd quarter of Hasta.

(d) Jupiter in deep exaltation in Lagna on days other than Saturday and Sunday.

Vidya Yoga—

(a) Friday when Pisces is rising and Venus occupies the 27th degree of the same sign.

(b) Jupiter in deep exaltation and Cancer rising on Thursday.

(c) The day and constellation being propitious, the Sun must be placed in his own Hora.

If education were to progress satisfactorily, one must have due regard to the following considerations also.

The forenoon and the noon are the best. Malefics should be disposed in the 3rd, 6th and 11th houses. The 8th house should be clean and unoccupied by benefic or malefic planets. For starting education, Wednesday morning would be the best provided the election chart is otherwise well disposed and strong.

Elections Pertaining to Education

Learning Vedas and Sastras.—Pushyami, Dhanishta and Sravana are auspicious ones. Let Jupiter be as strong as possible.

Learning Astrology and Astronomy.—Aswini, Punarvasu, Pushyami, Hasta, Swati, Moola and Revati are good.

Learning Grammar, Logic and Philosophy.—Rohini, Mrigasira, Punarvasu, Pushya, Hasta, Dhanishta and Revati are favourable constellations for learning Grammar while for the other subjects Sravana, Satabhisha, Hasta, Uttara, Moola and Revati are good. The intellectual planet Mercury should be fortified as usual.

Learning Medicine.—Dhanishta is the best constellation not only for beginning the study of medicine but also for learning the use of firearms. An affliction to Mars by Saturn should be avoided. Let the rising sign or Navamsa be that of Mars or the Sun.

To Learn Music and Dancing.—Let Venus be as strongly placed as possible avoiding affliction by Rahu or Saturn, as this is said to lead to an immoral career. Hasta, Pushyami, Dhanishta, Anuradha, Jyeshta, Revati, Satabhisha, Uttarashadha and Uttarabhadra are the best. Harmonious aspects should exist between Jupiter and Venus. Place the lord of Lagna in the 5th or 9th and see that these two houses are free from affliction. Mercury–Venus conjunction in Lagna would be highly propitious.

Learning any Science.—The Study of any science can be commenced either in a Saraswati Yoga or in a Vidya Yoga under any of the special combinations mentioned above.

Learning a Trade.—The planet ruling the avocation should be well disposed in regard to the ascendant and free from affliction. The following are the occupations governed by the different planets.

The SUN denotes kings, members of political department, ministers, magistrates, lawyers and civil servants. The Sun favourably situated in relation to the 10th house bestows professions of the above nature. The MOON rules over nurses, midwives, jewellers, dealers in pearls and precious metals, and also governmental activities. MARS produces soldiers, warriors, carpenters, mechanics, surveyors, chemists, bankers, commanders, insurance agents, and butchers. MERCURY gives rise to preceptors or school masters, mathematicians, authors, printers, secretaries, book-sellers, accountants and insurance agents. JUPITER makes one a priest, a lawyer, a councillor, judge, scholar and a public man. VENUS produces artistes, musicians, actors, perfumers, jewellers, wine-sellers and solicitors with a keen intellect. SATURN governs different kinds of professions involving responsibility and subordination, mill hands, compositors, hawkers, factory workers, scavengers and manual workers in general.

The planet in question may also occupy the 10th house aspected by benefics. Tuesday must be avoided for learning any trade.

CHAPTER XII

House Building

The instinct to possess a house is to be found not only in man, the acme of creation, but throughout the animal kingdom. The cells of bee's honey-comb are models of economy and mathematical skill while the ant-hills are noted for their strength. Man cannot be an exception to this primary instinct. Unfortunately, man, due to pride and arrogance, fails to give the thought and attention due to astrological factors which are as important as the selection of a site or planning of the building.

In Sanskrit, house-building goes under the name of *Vastu Shastra* and a lot of useful literature composed by great sages are extant on this most important subject. It must be within the experience of a number of persons that in spite of the best engineering skill displayed in the construction of a house, it would sometimes be lacking what is usually termed the 'charm' with the result the builder does not feel really happy at all. In India at least mere external appearance, however attractive, does not give the owner the mental satisfaction that a man of slender means enjoys when the house is built in conformity with astrological canons. So strong is the sentiment that even the most educated and "cultured" modern man would not afford to take risks in laying the foundation-stone or fixing the door-frame or entering the house without reference to astrological factors.

A house may look grand and attractive on the outside, may command and may possess all the appurtenances according to sanitary principles. Here the external factors, which we shall term the morphology of a house, are intact. But what about the internal or psychological factors involved? Every object in nature has the power of radiating *cosmic force* in some form or other. The materials collected for building a structure and the commencement of the structure itself involve the influx and interaction of a series of such invisible forces that the time selected should be capable of exerting forces harmonious to such invisible radiations. The ancient Maharshis had realised the importance of the interplay of such forces between objects in nature and man, though, in recent times, it has fallen to the lot of a Russian scientist and engineer, Georges Lakhovsky, to demonstrate its reality.

All objects in nature, whether mineral, vegetable or animal, are produced and destroyed under the influence of the solar ray and its various modifications. Many of the great buildings, intended for the use of an individual, community or a nation, have caused ruin to the parties concerned. It cannot be said that those buildings which have inflicted loss or ruin to the promoters of the schemes had no good engineering skill bestowed on them. When large sums of money are spent on such undertakings, it is natural to suppose that the best intellects in the field of engineering had been consulted and the greatest care had been taken in collecting proper materials. If the best heads and the best materials are used, it is natural to suppose that the results would also be most satisfactory.

On the contrary, we find that some buildings are spared the ruthless hands of time, some others crash very soon; some bring prosperity to the owner while some bring about unhappiness, misery and ultimate destruction. It cannot be an accident that while some buildings are spared the ruthless hands of wild conquerors, others close to them, or forming part and parcel of them, get destroyed under exceptional circumstances. There must surely be some reason for these variations in the ups and downs in the life of a building. The causes for these have to be searched far behind the superficial strata of argument and ordinary conception. The explanation is to be found in the great works on astrology composed by the sages.

If a construction is begun at a time when the strength of the materials is found in plenty—which can be ascertained by the rules of astrology, when the influences which work against the forces of cohesion; adhesion and chemical combination, etc., are counteracted by zodiacal and stellar influences, when the magnetic currents are favourable to the union and permanency of the materials, it is said to prosper long.

There is an important branch of astrology dealing with this absorbing subject under the name of *Vastu Sastra* and its study is very material to the securing of permanency and prosperity to the buildings constructed. The mysterious influence of time (Kalapurusha) is well marked. It accounts for the neglect or care of these buildings, their dilapidation or freshness, their occupation by men in power or by owls and other birds of ill-omen, their being covered up by mounds of earth or sand, and discovered after a long series of future generations to furnish facts and evidences for civilization which have disappeared, for societies which have passed away and for knowledge of construction which was concealed in the *Little Heads* which planned their commencement.

The combinations of planets at the time of commencement, the position and strength of constellation, the waning and waxing of the ever unsteady Moon, the rising or sinking of the principal designer, and the *Luck* of the party, who first lays the foundation-stone, have their own influence to exert.

The animal magnetism of the principle man has much to do with the prosperity of the edifice and also his heart and soul with reference to community who are to be profited by the construction. It is not astrology and sheer superstition when a lucky king or governor or president is asked to open an institution, to unveil a statue, to lay the foundation-stone for large buildings, and dig out a bit of earth for the success of the undertaking? These are the legitimate works of the humblest coolies, and if astrology has no hold, if influence of *Luck* has no place, why on earth do the most enlightened nations invite the luckiest man to open such proceedings?

Laying stones or digging the earth is not the legitimate function of any so-called big man. On the other hand, it belongs to the ordinary labourer who is present on the spot. If the most civilised nations of the earth do not believe in such *Nonsense* as luck and astrology, let them not be making themselves fools by resorting to such stupid ceremonies.

People are not frank. They do one thing and preach another. It is better that if they have no belief at all in the science of astrology they may not enact "tom fooleries" on ignorant and superstitious humanity.

House Building

The *Muhurtham* refers to auspicious combination of various planetary influences, and the *Worship* offered during such occasions before the work is commenced, has special reference to the averting of 'evils' which may be in store for the *Buildings* under question.

Astrology, as applied to engineering, goes under the special name of Vastu Sastra and merits deep study and understanding by modern engineers.

The construction of a house according to astrological works involves four important stages, *viz.*, (1) Laying the foundation, (2) Digging the well, (3) Fixing the door-frames, and (4) Entry into the new house. Of the four stages, the first and the last are very important and significant.

Laying the Foundation. — According to ancient astrological savants just as *Kalapurusha* personifies Time, *Vastu Purusha* personifies the House. The Vastu Purusha is said to sleep on his left with his head to the East during the months of Bhadrapada, Aswayuja and Kartika (August to October) ; with his head to the South during Margasira, Pushya and Magha (November to February) ; with his head to the West during Phalguna, Chaitra and Vaisakha (February to May) and with his head to the North during Jyeshta, Ashadha and Sravana (May to August). No building should be erected on the ground covered by his head, his legs, his hands and his back, as it is said to prove fatal to the father, wife and children respectively and cause fear of thieves. The most suitable section would be the ground covered by the stomach of Vastu Purusha as it gives rise to plenty and prosperity.

No house-building should be commenced in the lunar months of Jyeshta, Ashadha, Bhadrapada, Aswayuja, Margasira, Pushya and Phalguna as they connote respectively death, destruction, disease, quarrels and misunderstandings, loss of wealth, incendiarism and physical danger. The lunar months of Chaitra, Vaisakha, Sravana, Kartika and Magha are the best. The Sun should occupy fixed signs or at least movable signs but no building work should be undertaken when the Sun is in common signs.

Rohini, Mrigasira, Chitta, Hasta, Jyeshta, Uttara, Uttarashadha and Sravana are the best constellations to lay the foundation.

Swati, Pushya, Anuradha, Aswini, Satabhisha, Uttarabhadra and Revati are ordinary or middling while the remaining twelve asterisms should invariably be avoided.

All odd tithis (lunar days) except the 9th are good. Of the even tithis the 2nd, 6th and 10th are auspicious. Monday, Wednesday, Thursday and Friday are the best. Even Monday should be rejected when the Moon is waning. Sunday and Saturday are approved by some but in our opinion Saturday should be rejected as it connots frequent thefts. Sunday should also be avoided unless the day is otherwise very auspicious.

Fixed signs are the best. Movable signs should be rejected. Common signs may be preferred provided they are occupied by strong benefics. In movable signs and fixed *navamsas* can also be considered in cases of urgency, subject to the satisfactory disposition of other astrological factors. The rising sign at the time of laying the foundation should be highly fortified by the disposition of malefics in 3rd, 6th and 11th houses and benefics in kendras and trines. The 8th house should be vacant and in no case should it have the aspect of malefic planet.

The following are some of the special combinations recommended as highly propitious by ancient astrological writers for laying the foundation so that the house could last long and ensure happiness and prosperity to the owner as well as the tenant.

Foundation is to be laid in Cancer, the superstructure erected in Gemini or Virgo and the roofing done in Taurus or Libra. The house becomes fire-proof. A house built when Jupiter or Venus is in Lagna, and the Sun exactly on the meridian or at the western horizon, is supposed to last for at least one hundred years.

When the 10th house is occupied by the Moon, the 4th by Jupiter and the 11th by Mars and Saturn, the house will remain undestroyed for at least 80 years.

Jupiter in Lagna, Mercury in the 7th, Saturn in the 3rd, the Sun and Venus in the 6th, the house will stand for a century.

Mercury occupying Lagna, Jupiter the 7th and the Moon the 10th indicate similar stability.

Varahamihira suggests that after finishing the puja, the first foundation-stone shall be laid on the north-eastern corner of the site.

Fixing the Door-Frame.—The Hindus attach special significance to the fixing of door-frames. Even today the so-called educated man publicly scoffing at astrology stealthily consults an astrologer in private, and gets an auspicious time for fixing door-frames. Probably the door-frames have the peculiarity of attracting the best electric and magnetic forces from the atmosphere when fixed in auspicious times—times at which the different planetary bodies would be so disposed as to concentrate the maximum of benefic influence. The door-frame should always be fixed at a time when the rising sign is a fixed one. Rohini, Mrigasira, Uttara, Chitta, Anuradha, Uttarashadha, Uttarabhadra and Revati may be elected. The tithi (lunar day), asterism, the day and the rising sign should all be carefully selected, for the moment of fixing the door-frame has an important bearing upon the prosperity of the master. The doors, etc., may be furnished on Wednesday or Friday ruled by any beneficial lunar day, a common sign and any of the following constellations, *viz.*, Aswini, Pushya, Hasta, Rohini, Uttara, Uttarashadha and Uttarabhadra.

The durability or duration of a dwelling house in a state of prosperity should be determined from the moment at which the foundation-stone is laid. Foundations laid under the following combinations assure prosperity and a long life for the house to be constructed.

(1) From the Lagna, the Moon should be in the 10th; Jupiter in the 4th and Mars and Saturn in the 11th. (2) Jupiter in Lagna, Mercury in the 7th, Saturn in the 3rd, the Sun in the 6th and Venus in the 4th. (3) The rising sign should be occupied by Venus, the 10th house by Mercury, any kendra by Jupiter and the 11th by the Sun. (4) The Moon in the rising sign, Jupiter in the 7th and Mercury in the 10th. (5) Venus in the 10th, Jupiter in the 7th and Mercury in Lagna—which should be a fixed sign. (6) Jupiter in Lagna (fixed), Mercury in the 7th and the Moon in the 10th.

Any of the above planetary positions at the moment of laying the foundation will establish the building in prosperity for a long number of years.

Jupiter in combination with Rohini, Mrigasira, Aslesha, Uttara, Poorvashadha, Uttarashadha, Sravana and Uttarabhadra, on a *Thursday* forms what is known as Rajayoga and this is considered very fortunate for starting the construction of a house.

Digging Wells.—The object of sinking a well is to get a perpetual supply of clean and healthy drinking water. Varahamihira deals exclusively with the topic of divining the presence of water by reference to the growth of certain types of vegetation. The water falling from the clouds is soaked into the earth and according to internal conditions, runs into different channels. These channels of water are what are called under-currents. The type of vegetation present in the soil is said to give a clue to the distance of these under-currents from the ground level. For instance, Varahamihira says that if one sees a *Vetasa (Calamus viminalis)* plant in a waterless tract, one can find water by digging the ground at a distance of 3 cubits to the west of it, half a purusa (about $3\frac{1}{2}$ feet) below the earth. These can be easily tested by our water-diviners before condemning them as antiquated or superstitious. Soil conditions are influenced by climatic factors which in their turn have reference to planetary radiations. Therefore when wells are dug under favourable planetary conditions, a plentiful supply of water is expected without much expense.

Revati, Uttarabhadra, Hasta, Anuradha, Makha, Sravana, Rohini and Pushyami are favourable for digging wells. The rising sign should be Pisces, Cancer or Capricorn. Aquarius and Taurus will not give a good supply of water. Venus and the Moon should be in kendras. If the digging operation is begun in the sign occupied by the Sun, delay will be caused on account of the presence of hard-rock. An abundant supply of sweet water is indicated when the Moon or Venus is in a quadrant identical with a full watery sign. Venus and Moon are watery planets, while Cancer, Capricorn and Pisces (full) are watery signs.

Entering a New House.—If the house, which one has built, is calculated to give happiness to the family, one must take proper astrological counsel in entering it under a propitious moment. Soon after the eventful day—the day on which one's house is first occupied—if per chance something untoward happens, he will not only be heckled sarcastically by the family members, but his pride of possession disappears and he feels life not worth living though his sense of vanity would not allow him to own his short-sightedness.

Entering new houses will be a matter of great importance as the results produced by the local magnetic and electrical currents at the time of the entry of the family into it, may leave upon its members very far-reaching influences for good or bad. There is no mythology or superstition here. All human actions are productive of electrical currents.

"Vastu refers to the form of construction of the house, and the energies or forces called into existence by the arrangements made and the materials used in the construction. The subtle chemical results, effected by the conjunction of various materials, though not seen by the naked eye, are still there and any evil tendencies they may have, to produce danger, disease, or death to the occupants, must be very sensibly and dexterously neutralised or counteracted. Therefore the astrological works lay down certain principles and they are explained in the Mantra Shastra, where the processes by which those evil influences are averted are detailed at great length."*

New houses should be entered when the Sun is in Uttarayana, and when Jupiter and Venus are strongly disposed, after necessary worships and Bhootabali.

"Then term Bhootas is generally applied to represent the influences of the earth, fire, water, sky and air and the various compounds called into existence by their union. When special classes of materials and life beings

---
* *The Astrological Mirror* by Prof. B. Suryanarain Rao.

—including men and cattle—were absent from a particular plot or piece of ground the influences of the Bhootas (forces or energies) were naturally working in their own inscrutable ways.

"But the advent of new forms of energies or forces will certainly have their own influences and if the first set of Maha-Bhootas are found to be inimicable to the second set of forces, which are brought upon them for safety and prosperity, it becomes the duty of intelligent beings like men, to study the first set of physical and spiritual energies which had their permanent abode in them, so that the second set may not suffer from the "frowns" of the first set, and thus, have the very same objects defeated for gaining which men spent so much money, time and mental labour. Bhootabali therefore will be the special sacrifices which are enjoined upon men to offer to the Bhootas (forces) in the new house before they enter into the same and seek safety under its roof."

The lunar months of Vaisakha, Jyeshta, Magha and Phalguna are the best while Kartika and Margasira are neutral or middling. The most auspicious lunar days are the first of the dark fortnight, 2nd, 3rd, 5th, 7th, 10th, 11th and 13th of the bright half.

Rohini, Mrigasira, Uttarashada, Chitta and Uttarabhadra are the best constellations. Anuradha and Revati are also permissible. The other constellations should be rejected.

Monday, Wednesday, Thursday and Friday are auspicious. Saturday is also recommended by some Muhurtha writers, but there is risk of frequent thefts.

The Lagna or the ascendant should be a fixed sign. Common signs are ordinary while movable signs should be generally avoided. Provided, however, the Navamsa

Lagna is Taurus, a movable sign may be selected. The 8th house from the Lagna should be vacant.

Malefics should be disposed in Upachayas, benefics should fortify quadrants, the Moon must be strongly disposed and the rising sign should preferably be owned by Jupiter or Venus. When entry into a new house is effected under such a combination, prosperity and long life are said to be conferred on the person concerned. Griha Pravesam. done in one's own Janma Rasi, Janma Nakshatra or Janma Lagna, will produce highly beneficial results.

Griha Pravesam should not be done when the wife is in advanced pregnancy (above 6 months).

Buying Lands for Buildings.—The best asterisms for buying a land are Aswini, Rohini, Mrigasira, Punarvasu, Pushyami Uttara, Hasta, Swati, Anuradha, Uttarashadha, Sravana, Dhanishta, Satabhisha and Uttarabhadra. *Riktha tithis must be scrupulously avoided. Monday, Wednesday, Thursday and Saturday are good.

It would be better if the lord of the weekday concerned occupies the Lagna at the time of the transaction. Some ancient astrological works recommend Tuesday also as suitable. But in our humble view, Tuesday should be rejected.

At the time of making the final negotiations, let preferably a fixed sign rise and let Jupiter occupy a kendra or trikona. Mars should be placed in the 11th house and he should not be in Lagna. The lords of Lagna and the 7th should be harmoniously disposed. Avoid the 11th lord in the 12th.

The land can be taken possession of when the Lagna and Navamsa are occupied by the Sun and Ketu. When these planets are together in Lagna or Navamsa, the land is supposed to remain with the purchaser, permanently.

House Building

Buying Houses.—As usual Nanda* thithis are favourable. New and old houses can be purchased on Thursdays and Fridays. The auspicious constellations are Mrigasira, Aslesha, Makha, Pubba, Visakha, Moola, Punarvasu and Revati. Taurus, Gemini, Leo, Libra and Scorpio are the best signs. Malefics should be avoided in the 7th house, as they may cause trouble and annoyance. Mars should not be in Lagna.

Repairing Houses.—Do not commence repairs on Tuesdays. Friday at a moment when Lagna is Taurus or Libra and Monday when Cancer is rising are very suitable for beginning repairs. The Lagna must be occupied by a benefic and the Moon should be in an aquatic sign. Monday, Wednesday and Thursday are the best.

Walls can be whitewashed on Monday, Wednesday, Thursday and Friday. As usual, inauspicious lunar days and fiery constellations should be avoided.

No repairs should be started under the constellations of Krittika, Makha, Pushyami, Pubba, Hasta, Moola and Revati when Mars is transiting these constellations.

The most ideal combination either for laying the foundation or for entering houses or for buying and selling property is a Thursday identical with the presence of Jupiter in the following constellations:

Rohini, Mrigasira, Aslesha, Uttara, Poorvashadha, Uttarashadha, Sravana and Uttarabhadra.

Dismantling Buildings.—When you want to pull down a house, see that it is done on a day ruled by a fiery constellation preferably when the rising sign is movable. Then the Moon should be waning. Mars should be in an Upachaya. Avoid Thursdays, and the 8th, 9th and 30th lunar days.

---
* See appendix for explanation.

Removing to Another House.—This can be done when the usual *Tarabala* and *Chandrabala* are present, one's birth constellation would be propitious. Monday, Wednesday, Thursday and Friday are favourable. Saturday, Sunday and Tuesday should be rejected as also Riktha tithis or negative lunar days. If the house is taken for a purpose other than residential, then strengthen the Bhava or house denoting the purpose. Thus if the house is taken for investment purposes, see that the 11th house is strongly disposed. In any case an auspicious lunar day, a favourable constellation and a good weekday are very necessary so that the object in view may be gained.

CHAPTER XIII
Agriculture and Farming

The influence of planets on vegetation is an admitted fact. Frequent references appear in the writings of ancients and their knowledge gathered from observation and intuition is of inestimable value to us. It may be, the ancients realised that all manifestations of energy on earth of which we have knowledge are but the emanations of the cosmic rays. In fact according to Georges Lakhovsky "the concentration of matter and the appearance of life, both animate and inanimate, are but manifestation of these rays". Evidently the electro-magnetic forces radiated by the different planetary and stellar bodies have an intimate bearing on the origin and development of vegetable life. Solomon wrote: "There is a time to plant and a time to pluck up that which is planted; a time to kill and a time to heal". This is a sound astrological maxim.

Minerals, vegetables and animals form the worldly phenomena and this is admitted even by the most orthodox scientist. The interdependence of these three upon one another is too well known to need any elaboration. Behind these three grand kingdoms of nature are the agencies sent out by the solar globe. Under the solar agencies of sunlight, heat, sound, magnetism, electricity and other invisible agencies which are not yet discovered by the modern scientist but which were known to the ancient Maharishis, minerals grow, expand and crumble down. In their various states these minerals help the construction, growth, expansion and destruction of vegetables. Life pervades throughout the whole universe in some form or other, and all phenomena have life in them. Life as we conceive in men may be different from that found among the numberless animals, and then again among the countless varieties in the vegetable kingdom. Vegetables are produced by the minerals. Life functions are exhibited by all vegetation and every student of botany knows perfectly well that similarities exist between vegetable and animal functions—physiological, embryological, etc. Pushing on our natural law and analogy further the *life having* vegetables cannot be the products of *Lifeless* minerals. If evolution is a principle and theory recognised by experience then the life in the minerals will be in a particular stage, and with its environments and working under the great solar agencies of light, heat, sound, etc., it develops itself into a stage where it will be fitted to enter into the higher forms of existence among the various species of vegetables. Among the Ayurvedic texts, all the metals are said to have life and in converting them into powders *(Bhasmas)* there are great santhis or remedies prescribed which are considered to be effective in removing the sin which a doctor gets by killing and burning a *Loha* or metal. Thus it is clear that minerals beget vegetables and both are the product of solar energies manifesting themselves in a particular form. Spectrum analysis of light reveals that ultra-violet and infra-red rays mark the two ends of the spectral band. If a particular culture of bacteria is brought near the spectrum band, then such bacteria are found to collect near the red rays suggesting that the bacteria have a greater affinity towards the red rays. Similarly each kind of vegetable has an attraction for a particular type of planetary rays.

There is a direct and tangible connection between the planets and the vegetables. Constellations are bundles of electro-magnetic forces and their influences on crops are an admitted fact. Crops of various descriptions should be sown and reaped in certain constellations.

Cato (234-149 B.C.) gives us full assurance that "timber is felled most advantageously when the Moon is in conjuction with the Sun" and that "fig, apple, olive, and pen trees, as well as vines, should be planted in the dark of the Moon in the afternoon when there is no south wind blowing".

Plutarch (46–120 A.D.), in his commentary on Hesiod, asserts that the onion plant grows green and throws forth shoots during the waning Moon and dries up when the Moon is increasing.

The famous French Astronomer Camille Flammarion (1842-1925) testifies as follows : "Cucumbers increase at Full Moon, as well as radishes, turnips, leeks, lilies, horse radish, saffron". Herbs gathered while the Moon increases are of great efficacy. Varahamihira, the great astronomer and astrologer of the 1st century B.C., has made a very good study of vegetable astrology, and his observations deserve our careful attention.

Before dealing with the various Muhurthas for sowing seeds, grafting, planting, etc., I may casually refer to certain combinations of planets which denote, in a general manner, the nature of the different crops in the comming seasons.

If at the time when the Sun enters Scorpio, benefic planets should occupy the said sign, or the 4th, 7th or 10th from it. the *Greeshma* or summer crops will thrive well. The same result may be predicted, if Jupiter is in Aquarius and the Moon is in Leo. Summer crops will be good if at the time of Sun's entry into Scorpio, Venus or Mercury or both should occupy either Dhanus or Thula. If there are malefic planets on both sides crops will be injured. If a malefic occupies the 7th house at the time of Sun's entry into Scorpio, crops will suffer blight. If such 7th house is aspected by benefics, crops will no doubt be injured but they will not be totally destroyed.

Crops which grow in autumn will strive well or will be destroyed according as the planetary dispositions are good or bad at the time of Sun's entry into Taurus.

Buying Land for Agriculture.—Monday, Wednesday and Saturday are good. Let the Moon be waxing and Mars be in the 4th house. As usual, avoid the *Riktha tithis*. The best asterisms are: Aswini, Rohini, Mrigasira, Punarvasu, Pushyami, Uttara, Sravana, Satabhisha, Uttarabhadra, Vishitikarana may also be avoided. If due to any unavoidable circumstances, it is not possible to be present at the land to gain possession at the auspicious moment selected, then pick up and carry away a handful of earth from that land when Cancer is rising and the last pada of Bharani, Aridra or Visakha is ruling.

Ploughing the Land.—The soil should be tilled on days ruled by benefic planets. Generally, the sign Leo, or the sign occupied by the Sun or the constellation governed by him is favourable. The benefic stars are Rohini, Punarvasu, Pushya, Uttara, Hasta, Anuradha, Moola, Uttarashadha and Uttarabhadra.

All lunar days except the 4th, 6th, 8th, 9th and 10th and New Moon days are good. At the time of ploughing, let Taurus, Gemini, Cancer, Capricorn or Pisces be rising. Avoid Scorpio and Aquarius, if the rising sign is Mesha, it proves fatal to the cattle; if it is Scorpio, then crops will be destroyed by fire. If Aquarius, there is fear from thieves. See that the Lagna is free from malefic association. It is better that the bright half of the lunar month is selected.

On the first day start ploughing eastward or northward.

Sowing and Planting.—Any seeds can be sown on a day ruled by Hasta, Chitta, Swati, Makha, Pushyami, Uttara, Uttarashadha, Uttarabhadra, Rohini, Revati, Aswini, Moola or Anuradha provided the lunar day is also propitious. Choose a Lagna, owned by the planet who is lord of the weekday in question. Beets and carrots may be sown when the Moon is in Sagittarius. Potatoes and other underground vegetables should be sown when the rising sign is an aquatic one. On Thursdays fruit trées may be planted when Sagittarius and Pisces are rising. Flower seeds and cuttings may be sown in Taurus and Libra. Ragi, gingelli and all grains of black colour may be advantageously sown in Capricorn and Aquarius.

Always choose a Lagna owned by the planet who is lord of the weekday in question. Tomato may be planted while the Moon is waxing and is in the sign of Cancer. Capricorn rising is not favourable. For the best results the Moon should be waxing and the rising sign at the time of planting should be Cancer, Scorpio or Pisces. Generally speaking, seeds planted while the Lagna is Cancer tend towards abundance and fruitfulness. When the Lagna is Thula the yield will be smaller and the tendency is toward larger size in both fruit and flower. Aries: Garlic may be planted with success. Taurus: Peach, plum, potatoes, radishes, onion sets and turnips. Gemini: Not favourable for any planting being a barren sign. Cancer: Beans, cabbage, corn, cucumber, lettuce, melons, pumpkins, tomatoes, cauliflower, water-melons, and cereals. Leo : Not good for any planting, especially bad for underground plants such as potato. Virgo : Flowering plants. Libra : Wheat, rye, barley, rice and other field crops. Scorpio : Garlic and onion seeds. Sagittarius : Pepper and other spring crops and garlic. Capricorn : Potato, radishes and turnips. Aquarius : All black cereals and grains. Pisces : Cucumbers, pumpkins, radishes, water-melons and carrots.

All odd lunar days except the 9th are good. All even tithis except the 2nd and 4th should be avoided.

Seeds of flower plants, and fruit-bearing creepers should be sown in the asterisms of Mrigasira, Punarvasu, Hasta, Chitta, Swati, Anuradha and Revati. *Solanum indicum* grows under Bharani. Aswini is favourable for betal-nuts. Rohini is good for trees. Sugarcane grows well under Punarvasu. All varieties of grain thrive well under Pushya; Swati and Sravana favour paddy. Anuradha rules sesamum ; Moola is favourable for creepers and roots and black grain crops thrive well under Satabhisha.

Seedlings of coconuts may be planted in Aquarius. The following extract is from an ancient work on Muhurtha :

"Paddy should be sown on Sunday when the Sun is in Lagna ; seeds of flower plants (aquatic) should be sown on Thursday when Jupiter is in Lagna. Seedlings of flower sown on Tuesday when Mars is in Lagna ; Palmyra seedlings should be planted on Wednesday when Mercury is in Lagna. Seedlings of long-lived fruit trees should be planted on Thursday when Jupiter is in Lagna. Seedlings of flower trees should be planted on Friday when Venus is in Lagna. Seeds of black grains should be sown on Saturday noon when Saturn is in Lagna. While beginning all agricultural operations, see that the 8th house is unoccupied".

Grafting and Pruning.—Saturn should be favourably placed preferably in the 6th or 11th house. Strengthen the Lagna by placing a benefic in a kendra and by rendering the 8th house vacant. Avoid Tuesdays and Riktha tithis. In all agricultural operations, the position of the Moon is very important. See that the Moon is strong and free from affliction by Rahu, Ketu or Saturn. The Moon should be a benefic.

Felling Trees.—Trees should be cut when the Moon is in the last quarter so that the wood may be strong, massive and durable. The Lagna must be a dry sign aspected preferably by a dry planet.

Reaping the Crop.—Bharani, Rohini, Mrigasira, Aridra, Pushyami, Makha, Uttara, Hasta, Visakha, Anuradha, Uttarashadha and Sravana are favourable constellations to start reaping the crop. Avoid 4th, 8th, 9th, 11th, 12th and 14th lunar days as also the New Moon. Taurus, Gemini, Virgo, Libra, Sagittarius or Pisces should be rising.

Harvesting.—This can be commenced in Pisces Lagna on a day ruled by Bharani; Scorpio on a day ruled by Sravana; Cancer under Visakha. These pairs form special combinations and promote prosperity.

In-Gathering of Corn.—After the harvest is over, the produce has to be gathered in. This can be advantageously done under the constellations of Bharani, Rohini, Mrigasira, Pubba, Aridra, Punarvasu, Pushya, Makha, Uttara, Hasta, Swati, Anuradha, Moola, Sravana and Revati.

Saturn may be located in the 4th house. All lunar days except the 4th, 6th, 8th, 9th, 12th, 14th and New Moon are auspicious. Monday, Thursday, Friday and Saturday are good. The Amsas of Moon, Jupiter, Venus, and Saturn are also auspicious. Tuesdays and Sundays should be avoided. Movable signs must be rejected as they tend to destroy the grain by pests or decomposing.

Taurus rising on days ruled by Makha and Uttara respectively in the lunar months of Magha and Phalguna goes under the distinction of Dhanya Parvatha Yoga. Grain collected under this combination is supposed to confer happiness and prosperity to the person concerned.

Buying or Selling Cows.—Buying or selling of cows or cattle can be done under the constellations of Aswini, Punarvasu, Pushya, Hasta, Swati, Visakha, Jyeshta and Revati. Let preferably Taurus be rising. Avoid Mars in the 8th house.

Buying or Selling Horses.—Let the Moon and the lord of Lagna be friendly. Avoid their Dwirdwadasa relations. It is better that the transaction is done when Sagittarius is rising. Let the lagna be an airy sign if you wish to buy a race horse.

Buying Sheep.—Let the Lagna be Aries. Avoid Saturn in the 8th house. Let Aries or Capricorn be rising at the time of the transaction.

The Lagna and the 6th house should be strong when buying dogs or hounds. Birds should be purchased when the Lagna is an airy sign.

Any animal may be purchased on a Thursday ruled by Pushya when the Lagna is Aries. No animal should be sold on days ruled by Krittika, Aridra, Makha, Aslesha, Swati and Anuradha.

Intelligent, use of knowledge concerning planting, harvesting, breeding, etc., will bring satisfactory results. Disregard of these astrological principles is no excuse for failure.

CHAPTER XIV
Travel

Human nature varies from the highest genius to the greatest ignorance. Phenomena occur in nature whether we notice them or not. Dr. Johnson is said to have observed: "Let observation with extensive view survey mankind from China to Peru" Observing, reflective and thoughtful minds notice various phenomena, in their daily transactions of life which apparently seem to have no immediate connection with the failures and successes they meet with. But when carefully analysed it will be found that there is some sort of correlation between certain invisible agencies and events on the earth. But the true causes are intelligible to the ordinary minds. Suppose a man starts on an errand at an inauspicious time and fails in his mission, the planets are not to blame. They are only an index of events to happen. They merely reveal that influences operating when the man started on his mission were such as to give rise to failure. That the influence of time is not even or uniform needs no great explanation.

It must be within the experience of an intelligent man that solar heat and light differ at different times due to motion of the Sun. This is demonstrable to the ordinary senses. But there are invisible influences and agenices which can only be grasped by higher orders of intelligence. The ancient sages had been able to recognise these influences and how journeys undertaken at different times of year, month and day, would produce different kinds of results.

In the modern times, travel facilities have no doubt been perfected ; and so far as human conceptions go, the traveller is provided with every possible facility. But because the rules of astrology are ignored, there have been serious accidents and appaling loss of life. Man is incessantly subject to the bombardment of different kinds of forces emanating from planets and the interstellar spaces. The nature of the force operating at any given moment depends upon the nature of the disposition of the different planets at the moment concerned. Hence it can safely be pointed out that a journey undertaken at a propitious moment would enable the person to consummate the object in view and get back safely to his home. Instance of loss of life, loss of money, and distress and disappointments to the traveller, because the journey was undertaken when the planetary vibrations were inharmonious, can be cited *ad infinitum*.

A man wants to go to a foreign country on urgent business. Here he must have financial success, good health and a safe trip. We shall grant for argument's sake that at the time of starting, he is hale and healthy, has plenty of money and the travel agents have arranged for him the best conveyance. Naturally he may laugh at the idea that he should ever consult a good time for beginning his trip, when everything else is so very satisfactory.

The poor man must remember that the world's phenomena, physical and mental, are correlated and that the links between apparently two different and widely separated events, though invisible, are still present in the bargain and one who overlooks the currents of luck really omits important factors which may do him immense harm when he is least prepared to meet it. The laws of Nature, some visible and many invisible, are not controlled by the latest inventions or discoveries in the physical plane alone. The late Mr. Stead and 3000 men sailed on a ship that was constructed on the best scientific principles but an iceberg destroyed this Titanica with all the unlucky passengers in an hour or two. Lord Kitchner and his 600 officers were embarked on a splendid Man of War but at an unlucky hour and the whole crew were drowned within five minutes. We read in the daily press about the frequent occurrence of aerial, railway and automobile accidents resulting in the deaths of hundreds of innocent men, women and children. Many accidents can be prevented if due attention is paid to the *time-factor*. The most enlightened nations and persons have suffered the greatest calamities by sheer pride and prejudice and neglect of knowledge recorded by the intellectual gaints of past generations.

The ancients seem to have made a careful study of the subject of travel for various purposes and have framed sound astrological rules for the guidance of humanity. There is a vast literature extant on this subject. As usual. there has also been some difference of opinion between some of the standard texts. I have avoided all that is superficial and have confined myself to an elucidation of just the essential astrological principles governing travel or yatra.

Journeys.—The best lunar days are the 2nd, 3rd, 5th, 7th, 10th, 11th and 13th. The 14th lunar day and Full and New Moon days should be avoided at any cost.

If a journey is undertaken in the following constellations, the person is supposed to return back early after satisfactorily completing his work: Mrigasira, Aswini, Pushya, Punarvasu, Hasta, Anuradha, Sravana, Moola, Dhanishta and Revati. It is better that the journey is commenced in the 2nd, 3rd or last quarter of the constellation. The first quarter may be avoided as far as possible.

No journey should be undertaken on days ruled by Krittika, Bharani, Aslesha, Visakha, Pubba, Poorvabhadra and Aridra. Of these, the following nakshatras may be deemed fit for travelling beyond the spheres of evil influence :—Krittika—13 ghatis; Bharani—7; Makha—14; Pubba, Poorvashadha and Poorvabhadra—16; Swati, Aslesha and Visakha—14. In our humble experience, it is found that Bharani and Krittika should always be avoided while the other stars given in this paragraph, journeys can be undertaken in.

We have to emphasise that Bharani and Krittika should be invariably rejected.

Do not travel towards the East on Saturday and Monday; towards South on Thursday; towards West on Sunday and Friday and towards North on Wednesday and Tuesday. Provided the journey is timed to begin beyond 22 ghatis on Thursday, 12 ghatis on Tuesday and Wednesday; 15 ghatis on Friday and Sunday, 8 ghatis on Saturday and Monday, the above restriction does not hold good. In our view, Tuesday must preferably be avoided.

Aries, Taurus, Cancer, Leo, Libra and Sagittarius are favourable signs for starting on a journey.

Rising sign at the time of journey being one's Janma Rasi is highly favoured. But it should never be the sign of one's Janma Lagna. Journey should not also be undertaken when the Lagna is the 5th, 7th or the 9th from one's Janma Lagna.

Travel

Let Jupiter or Venus be well placed in Lagna at the time of starting. This makes the journey successful.

Ancient texts contain several other rules prohibiting journeys towards different directions when different constellations rule. There is then the question of Yogini, Chandra Garbha, Yatraphani Chakra, etc., a consideration of all of which would only lead to confusion. It is indeed very difficult to select a day thoroughly favourable in respect of all factors.

Therefore, readers would do well to restrict the choice of a day to considerations already set forth above. It must be noted that strict adherence to the astrological rules is impossible at times of emergency. Supposing a friend or relative is seriously ill and he is to be visited. There is no question of finding an auspicious date and time. The best thing to do is to begin the journey at the most auspicious hora of the day. If one is to go on a pilgrimage or on a pleasure trip or on business, arrangements for which could be made in advance, a day conforming to all astrological considerations should be fixed. The most essential factors to be remembered in selecting a suitable day for travel are (*a*) a good lunar day, (*b*) a favourable constellation, (*c*) a well-fortified Lagna and (*d*) the absence of Panchaka Dosha. If these are properly observed, that means all astrological precautions will have been taken.

The following general combinations would be of utmost importance to the average person:—

(1) Let the Moon be strong and dignified at the time of starting.

(2) Avoid days of vernal and autumnal equinox and the days on which the Sun enters a new sign every month.

(3) The Moon should be in the 3rd, 6th, 9th or 12th and Jupiter in a kendra from Lagna.

(4) Start when the Moon is in Lagna fortified by the disposition of Jupiter or Venus in a kendra.

(5) Jupiter strong in Lagna and the Moon in any place other than the 8th would be a strong combination.

(6) The journey will be easy and peaceful if the Moon be in the 7th and Venus and Mercury be in the 4th.

(7) Mercury in the 4th, Jupiter in the 2nd or 7th will neutralise all the other adverse influences.

(8) Benefics dignified in kendras of trikonas act as powerful antidotes for all evils.

(9) Jupiter in Lagna, malefics in Upachayas and Venus in any house other than the 7th would be an ideal combinations.

Short Journeys.—Render the Lagna and the Moon strong. If these two conditions cannot be fulfilled, start in the hora of the strongest planet keeping in view the Tarabala and Chandrabala factors.

Long-distance Journeys.—All the rules given in the earlier pages of this chapter are to be observed. Let the Moon be increasing and in a favourable situation so that there might be no delay or hindrance. Pay special attention to the eighth house and see that Mars is not there. Choose a day and time in which the Yatra Lagna agrees with the Janma Rasi. Avoid malefics in the 7th. If the journey is by car or train, avoid affliction to Lagna and the 8th lord by Mars and Rahu. If the Lagna is afflicted by Mars, there will be danger of accidents; if by Rahu, there will be disappointment and disease.

Pilgrimage.—Follow the rules in the earlier pages of this chapter. Let Jupiter be in Lagna or the 9th house. Avoid the months when Jupiter is combust.

Air Journeys.—Take due note of Tarabala. Let the Lagna be an aerial sign. Avoid Mars in Lagna, the 7th and the 8th. Let the Moon be waxing and as far away from Rahu as possible. Render the ascendant strong by a suitable disposition of Jupiter.

Sea Voyage.—Pay special attention to watery signs. Let preferably Cancer be the Lagna occupied by a watery planet. As usual, avoid Mars in Lagna, the 7th or 8th house. Venus should be favourably placed.

Business Journeys.—If you are to meet an influential person, let the rising sign fall in the 10th house in birth chart. Avoid malefics in Lagna and the 9th. Mercury is the planet of trade and business. He should therefore be either in Lagna or in the 10th or 11th but he should not be aspected by a malefic especially Saturn. Mercury in retrograde is also favourable as he will hasten the transaction to your satisfaction. Prosperity and success follow the Moon in good aspect to Mercury. If the Moon is in 8th or 12th house, the person falls ill on the way. Hence see that the Moon is in favourable position. See also that the 2nd lord is not afflicted and that he is favourably situated. In all these cases, mutual aspects between Mars, Saturn and Rahu should be invariably avoided as they indicate hitches and insurmountable obstacles.

CHAPTER XV

Medical Elections

The influences of the planets on human diseases appear with such persistence in the writings of the ancients that it is impossible to ignore their testimony in any orderly survey of the subject. While it is doubtless true that some of these references rest upon a basis of common superstition only, it is impossible to deny that many others appear to be founded upon careful observation and recorded experience.

The tithi and nakshatra, which are so important in Muhurtha, are based on the luni-solar movements. In the realm of astrology, the Moon is the sensorium, transmitter and collector of other planetary influences. In fact, seasonal changes, climate, electrical storms and our emotional behaviour are obviously correlated with the phases of the Sun and the Moon. Crises in acute diseases are marked by the transiting Moon which is the minute hand on the clock of destiny. The most serious crisis day in acute diseases is on the 14th day when the Moon is in opposition to his place when the disease started. When the Moon occupies certain positions, he disturbs the equalibrium of the patient's vitality so much so that medicine administered on such days would not prove efficacious. Hence the need for electing a proper time for undertaking medical and surgical treatments.

Medical astrology is a vast science and it is impossible to treat in this volume all the available information on the subject. Therefore I am giving such hints as would be absolutely necessary in the daily life of an average person.

Beginning Treatment.—If one is suffering from a chronic disease, the treatment should begin under Aswini, Rohini, Mrigasira, Punarvasu, Pushyami, Uttara, Uttarashadha, Uttarabhadra, Hasta, Chitta, Swati, Anuradha, Sravana, Dhanishta, Satabhisha, and Revati. In respect of ordinary complaints such as fever, biliousness, etc., no treatment would be necessary unless the person has fallen ill in Pubba, Poorvashadha, Poorvabhadra, Aslesha, Jyeshta, Aridra and Swati. Treatment is absolutely necessary when one takes to bed under the following combinations, *viz.*:—

(*a*) Sunday coinciding with the 4th lunar day ruled by Aridra, Aslesha or Makha.

(*b*) Tuesday coinciding with the 9th lunar day ruled by Jyeshta, Swati, or Bharani, and

(*c*) Saturday coinciding with the 14th lunar day ruled by Pubba, Poorvashadha and Poorvabhadra.

Similarly, an illness that sets in under one's Janma Nakshatra or the 3rd, 5th and 7th therefrom will cause much distress.

In regard to long-standing diseases or recurrent fevers, the best time for taking medicine is Monday, Wednesday, Thursday and Friday, coinciding with Hasta, Aswini, Chitta and Punarvasu respectively and especially at the time when the Moon, Mercury, Jupiter and Venus occupy their own vargas and a moveable Rasi or Amsa is rising.

Persons suffering from Typhoid or enteric should begin treatment on a Sunday coinciding with the 4th, 9th or 14th lunar day not ruled respectively by Aridra, Bharani and Visakha.

Any treatment commenced under Ugra yogas are supposed to prove successful. Ugra yogas arise when the 3rd (or 9th), 4th, 5th, 6th, 7th, 9th, 10th, 12th (or 3rd) and 13th lunar days coincide respectively with Rohini, Uttara, Sravana, Mrigasira, Revati, Krittika, Pushya, Anuradha, Krittika (or Makha).

Treatment for Venereal Disease.—Select a time when Aries or Cancer is rising on a New Moon day ruled by *Kshipram, Ugram and Chara constellations.

Treatment for Rheumatism.—The 3rd, 8th and 13th lunar days are good. Select Thursday ruled by Aslesha or Aswini.

Treatment for Gonorrhoea.—Wednesday is the best. Let the lunar day be the 4th, 9th or 14th ruled by Kshipra, Ugra or Chara constellations.

Treatment for Leprosy.—The rising sign should be Kumbha, Makara, Mesha, Simha or Vrischika. Place a powerful malefic in the 8th house. Select (*a*) Tuesday coinciding with Mrigasira, Chitta and Dhanishta, (*b*) Saturday ruled by Pushya, Anuradha and Uttarabhadra, and (*c*) Sunday coinciding with Krittika, Uttara and Uttarashadha. The lunar day must be the 4th, 6th, 8th, 9th or the 14th.

Treatment for Epilepsy.—Let the Lagna be a common sign or a moveable sign occupied by the Sun and the Moon. Fixed signs should be avoided.

Treatment for Consumption.—The lunar day must be free from Vishtikarana. The ruling constellation must

---
* See Appendix.

belong to the Sadharana group and the Moon must be aspected by a retrograde planet.

Treatment for Ascites.—Tuesday is the best. The constellation must be Bharani, Krittika, Aridra, Aslesha, Visakha, Makha or Jyeshta.

Taking Purgative.—Purgatives may be taken on the 2nd, 6th or 12th lunar day. Any weekday (except Tuesday) may be chosen provided the ruling constellation be Punarvasu, Revati, Swati or Aridra. Afternoon must be avoided.

Taking Enemas.—Select either Saturday or Tuesday and avoid malefic planets in the 7th and 8th houses.

Dental Treatment.—The Ugra yoga above referred to is quite suitable for dental treatment also. See that the Moon is not afflicted and that Chandrashtama is also avoided.

Taking Injections.—Injections may be taken on Saturday or Monday. Aries, Taurus, Cancer and Virgo are auspicious. The 8th house must be unoccupied. See that Mercury is free from affliction; as otherwise the pain will be severe and nervous weakness may set in.

Surgical Operations.—When possible, operate in the period of the increase of the Moon. Never operate at the exact time of the Full Moon as the bodily fluids are running highest then. Let not the Moon at the time of the operation be in the same sign as at birth. No operation should be done on the part of the body ruled by the sign through which the Moon is transiting at that time but wait a day or more until the Moon passes into the next sign below, and especially, if the Moon be in conjunction, or evil aspect to malefics at the time.

For surgical operations Tuesday or Saturday is recommended. Mars must be powerful. The 8th house should be unoccupied. And the ruling constellation is

Aridra, Jyeshta, Aslesha or Moola coinciding with the 4th, 9th or 14th lunar day. It is very necessary to strengthen the house ruling the part of the body to be operated upon. Thus if the stomach is to be operated upon, the time selected should be such as to render the 5th house strong by benefic aspects. Mutual aspects between Mars and Saturn should be avoided.

Treatment for the Nose.—The ascendant must be Cancer, Leo or Virgo. The Moon must be free from affliction. Avoid Mars or for that matter any malefic in the 8th. The Sun should be unaspected by Saturn or Rahu.

To Prepare Medicines.—Preparation of medicines should be commenced when the Lagna is Chara or Dwiswabhava. Fixed signs should be invariably rejected. The 6th, 7th and 8th houses should be unoccupied. Sunday, Monday, Wednesday, Thursday and Friday are good. Auspicious lunar days are the 1st, 4th, 6th, 8th, 9th, 11th and 14th.

Any panacea prepared when Saturn, Mars and the Sun are in Lagna or in a kendra from Lagna is said to become an effective remedy for all diseases.

Taking First Bath after illness.—When one has completely recovered from an illness of long duration, the first bath should be given on a day ruled by Aswini, Bharani, Krittika, Mrigasira, Aridra, Pushya, Pubba, Hasta, Chitta, Visakha, Moola, Poorvashadha and Poorvabhadra. There must be Tarabala also. Chandrashtamas should be avoided. Tuesday, Wednesday and Thursday are good. The 4th, 8th, 9th, 14th and New Moon days should be avoided.

CHAPTER XVI

Public Matters

In this chapter is included information on various matters concerning public welfare. In the light of the present official attitude towards astrology, this chapter cannot be of much practical importance. Yet as in several public functions in India astrological consultations are not altogether done away with but resorted to privately it is hoped that the principles given below would prove of value to those who are called upon to fix up suitable time for affairs of momentous importance to the public.

The astrological precepts on public affairs may be considered by ill-informed or half educated persons as ridiculous. But one who is a keen student of natural laws and who knows the importance of time and its manifestations cannot fail to notice that there is much sense underlying these precepts, for we are only asked to move in harmony with laws of nature. An intelligent man must question himself why, for instance a project launched at one hour proves fortunate investment. while another launched at a different hour proves most unluckly. Some ventures are doomed to failure from their very inception in spite of all the apparent favourable circumstances. Consequently even those who make it a point to scoff at astrology cannot help speaking such as "ill-starred affairs" although unaware of the meaning of this expression. Many nation-building activities have either proved abortive or resulted in failure simply because they were started in an unlucky moment.

Building and Launching Ships.—The constellations Jyeshta, Makha, Visakha, Aridra, Rohini, Bharani, Krittika and Aslesha should be avoided. The remaining ones are auspicious. Sunday, Thursday and Friday are good. Let the Lagna be a watery sign. Place the lord of Lagna in the 9th or 11th house. The lord of Janma Rasi should be in a watery sign. Avoid movable signs. Let there be no planet in 8th house. In building ships for war, strengthen the position of Mars. In building merchant and passenger ships, see that Mercury is dignified or at least occupies an Upachaya sign free from affliction. Either Venus or Jupiter should be in a kendra or trikona. The conjunction of Mars and Moon and Mars and Lagna or Lagnadhipathi should be avoided.

Building Towns and Cities.—The foundation stone should be laid at an auspicious moment as per rules given in the chapter on House Building. The best asterisms for laying the foundation for building a town are Aswini, Chitta and Revati. The Lagna must be a fixed sign powerfully aspected by Jupiter. This gives durability and continuance. Place Mercury in an auspicious position. This makes the city grow into a big trading centre. Confine Saturn to an Upachaya. Mars should have no connection with the Lagna. Have the construction begun when the Moon is increasing in light? Monday, Wednesday, Thursday and Friday are good. Movable signs should be avoided. Benefic planets should be in Lagna, the 2nd and the 9th houses. Malefics should be in 3rd and 11th houses. The 8th should be vacant as also the 12th. But a benefic in the 12th is permissible.

Building Military Quarters.—The constellation of Uttarabhadra is the best for beginning the construction of military quarters or barracks.

Dairy Farms.—Let Taurus or Cancer be the rising sign. Aswini, Punarvasu, Pushya, Hasta, Swati, Sravana, Dhanishta and Satabhisha are the best Nakshatras. The presence of the Moon in Lagna augurs prosperity. Monday is the best weekday.

Electing Head of the State.—The best constellations are Aswini, Rohini, Mrigasira, Punarvasu, Pushya, Uttara, Hasta, Anuradha, Uttarashadha, Sravana, Uttarabhadra and Revati. All odd lunar days (in the bright half) except the 9th are good. The 2nd and 10th lunar days are also favourable. The rising sign must be Aries, Taurus, Gemini, Cancer, Leo, Sagittarius, Aquarius or Pisces.

Strengthen the Sun and the Moon. Fortify the Lagna and the 10th and their lords. Let the 8th house be vacant. Confine malefics to Upachayas. If possible, the Sun and the Moon should be placed in Cancer or Leo preferably subject to the aspect of Jupiter. As usual, the *Tarabala, Chandrabala, Panchaka*, etc., should be carefully looked into.

Coronation.—The foregoing rules apply to coronation also. If possible, let Lagna be Leo occupied by the Sun and aspected by Jupiter. In case of democratic rule, the new Government may begin at a time when Kumbha is rising with Saturn in Lagna or in Thula aspected in either case by Jupiter or Venus.

Installing a Deity.—Building temples and installing deities involve the consideration of very important astrological principles which an average student of astrology will be unable to understand thoroughly. Therefore, selection of an auspicious moment for such purposes may well be left to a specialist. There are complicated astronomical, astrological and religious rules given in original works and the reader will do well to refer to such works as *Brihat Samhita*, *Kalamrita*, etc., for greater details. Here I shall give just a few salient principles.

The installation of a deity should be done when the Sun is in the Northern course. The lunar month of Magha should be avoided. According to *Kalaprakasika*, the ceremony is to be done when Jupiter and Venus are dignified and devoid of adverse influences.

Rohini, Mrigasira, Punarvasu, Pushya, Uttara, Hasta, Swati, Uttarashadha and Uttarabhadra are good constellations for this purpose. All odd lunar days (except the 9th) including the 2nd, 6th and 10th are favourable. The Lagna must be a fixed sign. A common sign may be selected for a female Deity. Movable signs should always be rejected. The Lagna should not be conjoined by the luminaries or malefics or otherwise the town concerned will be destroyed. No malefic should occupy the 7th. There should be no planet in the 8th. The ceremony should be avoided at the end of an Ayana, the end of a year, of a lunar day and of an asterism; and on days on which halos round the Sun and the Moon are visible.

CHAPTER XVII

Miscellaneous Elections

In the foregoing chapters elections bearing upon almost all human activities have been clearly described. In this chapter I propose to deal with a few more important ones bearing upon sports, law-suits, prisoners and war.

Lotteries and Competitions.—Success in lotteries and competitions generally depends upon the strength of the birth horoscope in regard to the house of finance and the nature of the directional influences at the time concerned. Therefore, much reliance cannot be placed on the strength of election in regard to chance-games.

Aswini, Bharani, Punarvasu, Pushya, Hasta, Chitta, Visakha, Poorvashadha and Revati are excellent for entering into competitions. The 2nd, 3rd, 5th, 6th, 11th and 13th lunar days are good. All weekdays are suitable except Tuesday and Saturday. Let the Lagna belong to a benefic planet. Fortify the Moon and the 5th and the 9th houses. Avoid the 11th lord in the 12th and Mars in the 8th. Saturn should cast no aspect either on the 2nd house or on the 2nd lord.

Horse Races.—Here again the birth chart is important. Horses are said to be governed by Aswini. This constellation therefore is fortunate for purchasing and training a horse for race purposes. Krittika, Mrigasira, Punarvasu, Pushya, Uttarabhadra, Hasta, Swati, Visakha, Anuradha and Dhanishta are also good. Monday, Wednesday, Thursday and Friday are favourable. If you want to run a horse for a race, place Sagittarius in Lagna and strengthen the 10th house.

Filing Law-suits.—Avoid the usual unfavourable lunar days. Aswini, Rohini, Mrigasira, Pushya, Uttara, Hasta, Chitta, Anuradha, Dhanishta and Revati are good. Tuesday and Saturday should be avoided. Strengthen the Lagna by placing Jupiter in a Trikona. Let there be no malefic in the 6th house. The lords of Lagna and the 6th should be as far apart as possible. The Lagna or at least the Navamsa must be Aries in order to assure success to the litigation. If benefics occupy kendras or occupying the male signs, have beneficial aspects, there will be peace between the parties.

Seeking Escaped Prisoners.—Saturday, Monday and Tuesday are favourable weekdays. Aswini, Rohini, Aridra, Aslesha, Pubba, Chitta, Visakha, Moola, Uttarashadha and Revati are auspicious. The Lagna must be in a movable sign aspected or occupied by Mercury or Moon. The 6th lord should occupy the 11th and be free from affliction. See that the Moon does not occupy the 12th in conjunction with any other planet. Make the Sun weak. If possible, let Rahu or Ketu be posited in Lagna. Parivarthana or exchange of house between lords of Lagna and the 7th is also desirable.

Buying Arms.—The most favourable constellations are Punarvasu, Pushya, Hasta, Chitta, Rohini, Mrigasira, Visakha, Anuradha, Jyeshta, Uttara, Uttarashadha, Uttarabhadra, Revati and Aswini. Avoid *Riktha Tithis* the 4th, 9th and 14th lunar days. Sunday, Thursday and Friday are auspicious. Some works recommend Tuesday also as favourable. A martian sign must be rising or culminating and Mars must be in a dignified position.

Starting Wars.—Several standard works on Muhurtha do not specially mention the constellations, etc., suitable for starting wars. Planetary combinations for the defeat of the enemy are given. However, by a reference to relevant literature on the subject, we have been able to gather the following information. War must be started on a day ruled by Aswini, Bharani, Krittika, Aridra, Aslesha, Makha, Pubba, Chitta, Jyeshta, Satabhisha and Revati. Of the lunar days except the 4th, 9th and 14th the rest are said to be fortunate. Sunday, Tuesday and Thursday are supposed to ensure victory.

In our humble view if Tuesday is selected Mars must be rendered strong.

The enemy is said to retreat in confusion if the war is begun in a Chara Lagna when the Moon occupies a fixed sign. The enemy is also said to retreat early if the Lagna is Aries, Leo, Taurus and Sagittarius. There should be no conjunction of or aspect between Mars and Saturn if great mortality and bloodshed are to be avoided. Mars should be elevated preferably in the 7th house or the meridian unaspected by any other malefic. The Lagna must, as usual, be strong.

Destroying Strongholds.—Let a fiery sign be rising with Mars posited in or aspecting Lagna. A strong-hold besieged under the influence of Aries is bound to fall early. Similarly, Sagittarius ascending with Mars in it would render the collapse of any stronghold inevitable.

Making Peace.—This is an important item in the lives of nations. Peace must be under a strong influence of Jupiter. The ascending sign and amsa must be either Pisces or Taurus or Virgo. Benefics should be strongly placed. Saturn must be either in the 12th or in Upachaya. There should be no conjunction between Mars and Rahu or Mars and Saturn or Rahu and Saturn. The signatories to the Peace Treaty must themselves have their horoscopes harmoniously disposed. The constellations of Mrigasira, Chitta, Dhanishta, Aridra, Swati, Satabhisha, Anuradha and Uttarabhadra should be avoided, as also the 4th, 7th, 8th, 9th and 12th lunar days and New and Full Moon days. Peace made under the following combinations is said to last for a long time :—

(1) The Moon should be in the 10th house, Jupiter in the 4th and Mars and Saturn in the 11th (Mars and Saturn should not be in conjunction).

(2) Jupiter should be in Lagna, Mercury in the 7th, Saturn in the 3rd, the Sun in the 6th and Venus in the 4th.

(3) Jupiter should be in the 5th from Lagna (which should be Taurus), Sun in the 3rd and Mars in the 6th.

(4) Mercury in Lagna, Jupiter in the 7th and the Moon in the 10th.

(5) Jupiter in Lagna (which should be a fixed sign), Mercury in the 7th and the Moon in the 10th.

Will our statesmen pay heed to the astrological counsel and try these simple astrological rules and rid the world of perpetual threat to Peace?

The conceit of modern progress has no more respect for ancient ideas than for the forgotten civilizations of old, even though in many essentials they have anticipated or outstripped all that we boast of.

CHAPTER XVIII

Summary

In the last seventeen chapters, we have been able to cover almost all the important aspects of Muhurtha, a branch of astrology which is still very popular amongst all sections of people not only in India but in other parts of the world too.

The rationale of Muhurtha consists in appreciating the importance of the time-factor in all human undertakings. It is an admitted fact that all source of life and terrestrial activities is the Sun. Forces emanating from this glorious body vary in intensity and influence as a result of their contact with other celestial bodies. Man is himself a bundle of electrical currents and therefore there is always a sort of interaction between planetary forces and those incessantly radiated by man. By Muhurtha is meant that valuable moment when there is the greatest harmony or resonance between human and stellar radiations.

Horoscopy is diagnostic. Muhurtha is preventive or prescriptive. It sets at naught the theory of absolute determinism and gives scope for the display of volition within reasonable limits. Therefore even if afflictions exist in the birth horoscope they can be neutralised or at least lessened by recourse to Muhurtha.

Muhurtha takes into cognizance the importance of the radical Moon as he indicates the mind and all our psychological inhibitions. Hence almost every election is to be so timed as to have reference to the birth star and consequently to the birth Moon. Janma Tara is the ruling constellation while Janma Rasi means the zodiacal sign occupied by the Moon at the time of one's birth.

In electional astrology, the *Panchanga*, made up as it is of five important astrological limbs, is of great significance. The Panchanga consists of (1) Tithi, (2) Vara, (3) Nakshatra, (4) Yoga and (5) Karana.

The Tithi is the lunar day. This can be known thus: Subtract the longitude of the Sun from that of the Moon in degrees at a given time. Divide the remainder by 12 and the quotient *plus* one will be the current tithi. The remainder when subtracted from 12 and divided by the diurnal motion in degrees will give in-day the time at which the lunar day will change. *Vara* is of course the usual weekday commencing from Sunday and ending with Saturday. The *Nakshatra* is the ruling constellation. This can be ascertained thus :—Reduce the position of the Moon into minutes and divide it by 800. The quotient represents the past nakshatra and the remainder as portion of the next star. Then we have the *Yoga* which may be obtained thus :—Take the position of the Sun and the Moon and divide it by the sum of their motions. The quotient as usual represents the past yoga. Then we have the last limb, *viz.*, Karana or half a lunar day. There are 27 Nakshatras, 27 Yogas and 11 Karanas.

In Muhurtha, the pride of place is always given to Nakshatra, Vara and Tithi. The other two limbs whilst no doubt important in their own way are in actual practice of secondary value.

In selecting auspicious times, due notice must be taken of the purpose in view. Each human activity requires the strengthening of a particular house or

Summary

signification or the presence of a particular type of combination.

Rasis and constellations have their negative periods also. Such periods should be rejected in all good works. Tuesday and Saturday are invariably bad for all auspicious works. There are certain exceptions for this general rule. For instance, Tuesday is good for surgical operations.

The most important factors to be considered are the Tarabala or strength of constellation, Chandrabala or lunar strength and the Panchaka or the strength of the sum-total of five kinds of energies called into play at a particular moment. In all these cases there are exceptions to be noted. Hence, in the election of a Muhurtha, one should be very careful. Each constellation has its own role to play as suitable for a certain type of activity. In fact, Pushyami is considered a constellation *par excellence*. It could be employed for all purposes but not for marriage.

There are twenty-one great evils (Mahadoshas) being the resultant of the operation of the various forces. As many of these doshas as possible must be avoided. Of these, Kujashtana and Bhrigushataka are definitely harmful for marriage while the others are equally evil in respect of other elections. One important consideration should weigh with the Astrologer, *viz.*, that the force of good must supersede those of evil for an absolutely good Muhurtha is inconceivable. Several combinations and exceptions are given which would render the forces of evil either null and void or less harmful. For instance, no day of the week is blemished provided the lord thereof is strongly placed. A benefic exalted in Lagna should nullify all other adverse influences. If the kendras are fortified, sources of evil are considerably lessened.

A certain weekday coinciding with a certain lunar day and constellation constitutes a special Yoga capable of generating very good influences. For example, Thursday identical with the 4th lunar day and the constellation Makha gives rise to Siddha Yoga, a highly favourable combination. These special influences merit the attention of a student of Muhurtha.

Of the Shodasa Karmas (16 kinds of ceremonies) prescribed for the Hindu, excepting a few, the rest are common to persons of all castes, creeds and nationalities and they are therefore of universal application. Nishekam or the first sexual act is astrologically very significant for *"not only do the radiations from these stars exercise an influence on the animal and human embryo but, since all substance, living or inert, is constituted of elections which are materialised radiations, the formation of all organic beings on earth depends directly on the influence of these radiations on the human egg at the moment of conception".

The ancients have also hinted at the possibility of change of sex by having the ceremony of Pumsavana done when the foetus has attained a certain age. Of the post-natal ceremonies, Upanayana is very important. Fixing a suitable time for this ceremony is indeed highly difficult. This should be left to be done by an expert until the student has gained sufficient experience which could enable him to do the work independently.

In regard to marriage, the following suggestions may be carefully noted:—

(1) Do not begin the comparison of horoscopes without testing the correctness of the castings submitted.

(2) Examine the longevity of the bridegroom and the bride. If short life is indicated either for the bride

---
* *La Grand Problem* by Lakhovsky.

or for the bridegroom do not recommend the match unless there are neutralising influences in either of the horoscopes.

(3) The 7th and 8th houses should be carefully examined. When there are many afflictions, carefully find out if there are neutralising influences also. Otherwise reject the match.

(4) The first condition is the inherent strength of the horoscope. Next in importance comes the question of examining marriage adaptability.

(5) A girl belonging to Rakshasa Gana should not be married to a boy belonging to Manusha or Deva Gana. The reverse condition is recommended.

(6) In examining Graha Maitra which is the *sine qua non* of marriage stability, consideration should be had not only to the Janma Rasis of the couple but to the Janma Navamsa also. When Graha Maitra does not exist according to Janma Rasi, then the latter must be considered. Under certain conditions (p. 91) even want of Graha Maitra can be ignored. All these have to be carefully looked into before pronouncing an opinion. The common Janma Nakshatra factor presents many difficulties for a beginner in astrology. The subtle distinctions bearing on this consideration should be carefully grasped. Then there is the question of Kuja Dosha about which much fuss is being made in this part of India. No horoscope should be rejected unless it has been examined from all astrological angles.

(7) If the girl and the boy have their 5th houses considerably afflicted, then marriage between them is not desirable. But much of the evil due to these radical dispositions can be overcome by selecting a proper Muhurtha

(8) *"In the beginning of your literary attempts in the astrological field do not be over-confident or hasty in having properly understood the principles explained here. Refer your knowledge to some gentlemen who have much experience in these matters and whose opinions you ought to value and compare with your inferences and personal experiences".

(9) In marriages, there should be no three or more *Jyeshtas*. The eldest son or daughter is called a Jyeshta. There is the lunar month of Jyeshta and the constellation of Jyeshta. Therefore the marriage of an eldest son or daughter should not be done in the constellation of Jyeshta and the lunar month of Jyeshta. Similarly if the bride and bridegroom happen to be Jyeshtas the marriage should not be celebrated either in the month of Jyeshta or in the constellation of Jyeshta.

(10) In fixing a Muhurtha for marriage, keep the 7th house clean, and 6th and 8th unoccupied by Venus and Mars respectively. Jupiter's presence in a kendra or trikona is very desirable.

(11) When birth data are not available, take the Nama Nakshatra (see Appendix) of the couple. The name of an individual is made up of letters or aksharas, by which is meant indestructible forms of sound vibrations, and when you consider a name, you are only measuring the energy content of the individual.

(12) Parents waste huge sums on *Marriage Shows* such as dinners, music, jewels and pandals but they are niggardly in paying proper remuneration to a deserving astrologer who could fix up a really auspicious moment. If astrological consultation is not to be a matter of formality but of serious importance, then the learned

---

* *The Astrological Mirror* by Prof. B. Suryanarain Rao.

astrologer should be paid properly. A proper Muhurtha will ensure the future of the couple and anything expended towards this item is well spent. If without caring to consult an expert astrologer, the marriage is done and it proves a failure, then all the energy and finance spent would be a sheer waste. Hence it is very necessary that an expert astrologer is pressed into service.

General elections given in Chapter XIV comprehend very important human activity and as far as possible due attention must be paid to the astrological factors either in regard to going on a journey or starting a business or for doing any important work. Auspicious times for day-to-day activities can be fixed by any amateur astrologer.

Astrology in relation to house building is a very important subject, as it takes into account factors which the architect and the engineer generally ignore. Materials assembled for the construction of a building radiate different kinds of energies some good, some indifferent and some definitely harmful. Force of evil accruing from such sources can be tapped off by laying the foundation-stone and entering the new house at propitious moments. An amateur astrologer should not take the responsibility of doing this job as it pre-supposes very intimate knowledge of Vastu Sastra.

In the matter of Travel or Yatra, Krittika, Bharani and the lunar days of Ashtami and Navami should be invariably avoided. Journeys are also prohibited towards different directions on different weekdays. There are exceptions for such rules in cases of emergency. In selecting a suitable day for travel, a good lunar day, a favourable constellation and a well-fortified Lagna merit one's foremost attention. For short journeys existence of Tarabala is enough. For going on pilgrimages or important errands, a very suitable day has to be fixed by taking due note of all the important astrological factors.

The medical elections are intended to ensure speedy recovery from illness. There is a striking correspondence between the lunar movements and crises in certain types of disease and this gives a clue as to why a suitable time should be secured to commence treatment for long-standing diseases and surgical operations. Generally Monday, Wednesday, Thursday and Friday coinciding with Hasta, Aswini, Chitta and Punarvasu respectively would be highly favourable to begin treatment for recurrent fevers and chronic diseases. The time becomes specially propitious if in addition to the above the Moon, Mercury, Jupiter and Venus occupy their own vargas and a movable Rasi is ascending in Amsa.

Elections bearing on public matters are of dubious value in view of the current prejudicial official attitude entertained towards astrology. Yet, as in actual practice, astrologers are being consulted in private for official purposes, the rules bearing on elections pertaining to public affairs are bound to be of some value. It is hoped the day is not far off when astrology is given its due by the State and recognised as the science *par excellence* for the solution of national and international problems. This expectation on our part may induce a derisive laugh from "men of sobriety" whose habit of thinking is confined to a limited horizon. But we are bold enough to say that astrology when properly pressed into the service of the State would be far more useful in preventing national and international complications than all the paraphernalia now employed by the civilised Governments all over the world.

Concluding Remarks

Muhurtha is not the penance for all the ills afflicting a horoscope. Muhurtha or an auspicious moment can neutralise to a certain extent the afflictions existing in a birth chart as affecting the various events.

If marital harmony is completely absent in a birth chart, Muhurtha cannot confer on the native marital harmony. It reduces the sources of friction to a certain extent.

Of the different limbs of the *panchanga*, *viz.*, *tithi*, *vara*, *nakshatra*, *yoga* and *karana*, the nakshatra is very important. If suppose for a marriage, the tithi is the 6th and the nakshatra is Sadhana, then the day can be selected. This is the view of sage Brihaspati and hence acceptable to the other sages. But even if other factors such as *tithi*, *nakshatra*, etc., are defective, a strong Lagna can neutralise such defects. This is the view of Narada and we concur with this view. But recourse should be had to this contingency only under special circumstances, *e.g.*, when a Muhurtha is to be fixed, say for accommodating a bridegroom coming from a foreign country, who has to get back quickly.

*According to Roua, Jupiter should be rendered strong for marriage ; Venus for travel ; Mercury for learning ; Mars for war, fighting ; the Sun for meeting with the rulers, government officers, etc., and the Moon in respect of all elections.

---

* गुरुर्विवाहे गमने च शुक्रो
ज्ञाने बुधौ दीक्षणके च सौरिः ।
रणेषु भौमो नृपदर्शनेऽकं:
सर्वेषु कार्येषु शशी बलाढ्यः ॥

Abhijin Muhurtha (midday) could be fixed for all elections, in case a really auspicious time is not available. Add half duration of the day to sunrise and the Abhijin Muhurtha is obtained. Suppose sunrise is at 6-10 a.m. (IST) and sunset 6-45 p.m. The interval is 12 hours 30 minutes. Half this, *viz.*, 6 hours 15 minutes added to time of sunrise, *viz.*, 6-10 (IST) gives the Abhijin Muhurtha as 6 hours 10 minutes + 6 hours 15 minutes = 12 hours 25 minutes.

[1]According to Sage Bharadwaja, a fully flawless Muhurtha is unthinkable for years. Therefore, fix up an auspicious time, with less *doshas* and more *gunas*. Even sage [2]Narada says: Avoiding heavy afflictions (mahadoshas), and considering the ordinary gunas and doshas, fix an auspicious time with more gunas. That moment proves auspicious.

And always see that [3]Jupiter or Venus is in conjunction with the ascendant or at least in a kendra or the trine so that all doshas are rendered infructuous.

The sages appear to have taken a very liberal view of things especially in regard to marriage. For instance they say that if the boy and the girl like each other in their first meeting, that should also receive first consideration—मनोनुकूलं प्रथमं प्रशस्यं । And when doubts arise between views of different astrologers about the

---

[1] दोषान् सर्वान् परित्यज्य न शक्यं बहुवत्सरैः ।
तस्मात् परीक्ष्य कर्तव्यमल्पदोषं गुणाधिकम् ॥

[2] महादोषान् परीत्यज्य शेषयोर्गुण दोषयोः ।
गुणाधिक स्वल्पदोषः सकालो मगलप्रदः ॥

[3] तिथेश्च ग्रहवारादौ ये योदाशास्त्रोदितः पुरा ।
ते सर्वे नाशामायांति जीवशुक्रे क्षणोदयोः ॥

agreement of horoscopes, we are asked to have recourse to *nimitta* (omens) and clinch the issue.

The outstanding exponent of astrology in 20th century was my revered grandfather the late Prof. B. Suryanarain Rao, a great historian, savant, linguist and philosopher. Prof. Rao successfully defended astrology against the attacks of ill-informed critics most of whom belonged to the so-called "educated" classes. I conclude this work with the following extract from the late Professor's *The Astrological Mirror* :

"To despise to hold a bright lamp in the darkness indicates stupidity, while to try to secure it at any cost and hold the same to shed light on our future path really shows consummate wisdom. Choose your own lot as you please, and either control the planets and stand a victor in the struggle for existence and comfort or yield to their evil influences without personal exertions on your part and be a miserable coward."

Om Tat Sat

APPENDIX I

Afflicted.—A planet that is aspected by or is associated with malefics.

Apoklimas.—The 3rd, 6th, 9th and 12th.

Benefics.—The waxing Moon, well-associated Mercury, Jupiter and Venus.

Conjunction.—According to Hindu Astrology, if two planets are in the same sign, they are said to be in conjunction.

Debilitation.—Position that weakens the influence of a planet. All planets get debilitated in 180° from their exaltation points.

Equinox, Vernal.—The day on which the tropical Sun crosses the first point of Aries. This will generally be 21st March every year.

Equinox, Autumnal.—The day on which the tropical Sun crosses the first point of Libra. This will generally be 21st September.

Exaltation.—Positions that strengthen the influences of a planet. The Sun, the Moon, Mars, Mercury, Jupiter, Venus and Saturn respectively are exalted in Aries 10°, Taurus 3°, Capricorn 28°, Virgo 15°, Cancer 5°, Pisces 27° and Libra 20°.

Fortify.—To render the zodiacal position strong by directing on its aspects from benefic planets or by positing benefic planets in certain angular positions.

Houses.—A horoscope has 12 houses comprehending all important human events. The affairs under the various houses are as follows :—

1st House.—Build, body, appearance.

2nd House.—Family, source of death, property, vision.

3rd House.—Intelligence, brothers, sisters.

4th House.—Vehicles, general happiness, education, mother.

5th House.—Fame, children.

6th House.—Debts, diseases, misery, enemies.

7th House.—Wife or husband, death, tact.

8th House.—Longevity, gifts.

9th House.—God, Guru, father, travels, piety.

10th House.—Occupation, karma, philosophical knowledge.

11th House.—Gains.

12th House.—Loss, moksha.

Kala Purusha.—Time Personified.

Karanas Unfavourable.—Vishti, Chatushpada, Naga, Kimsthugna and Sukuna.

Kendras.—The 1st, 4th, 7th and 10th.

Maharshis.—Great sages of India.

Malefics.—The waning Moon, Mercury with evil planets the Sun, Saturn and Mars.

Moolatrikonas.—Positions similar to exaltation.—The Sun, the Moon, Mars, Mercury, Jupiter, Venus and Saturn have their Moolatrikonas respectively as Leo, Taurus, Aries, Virgo, Sagittarius, Libra and Aquarius.

Muhurtha.—This is one of the important branches of predictive astrology having mainly to do with the election of favourable time for different human activities.

Nakshatras, Types of—Vajra or Kshipram—Bharani, Makha, Pubba, Poorvashadha and Poorvabhadra. Theekshna or Ugram—Aridra, Jyeshta, Aslesha and Moola. Laghu—Aswini, Pushya and Hasta. Mrudu—Mrigasira, Chitta, Anuradha and Revati. Sthira—Rohini,

Uttara, Uttarashadha and Uttarabhadra. Chara—Punarvasu, Swati, Sravana, Dhanishta and Satabhisha.

Namanakshatra, Finding.—Namanakshatra means the constellation due to one's name. In the absence of birth data, this is very necessary. Each constellation has been given four letters to be taken as 1st, 2nd, 3rd and 4th quarters.

1. चु, चे, चो, ला — अश्विनि
   ಚು, ಚೆ, ಚೋ, ಲಾ — ಅಶ್ವಿನಿ
   Chu, Chey, Cho, La — Aswini

2. लि, लु, ले, लो — भरणि
   ಲಿ, ಲು, ಲೆ, ಲೋ — ಭರಣಿ
   Li, Lu, Ley, Lo — Bharani

3. आ, इ, उ, ए — कृत्तिका
   ಆ, ಇ, ಉ, ಎ — ಕೃತ್ತಿಕಾ
   Aa, Ee, U, A — Krittika

4. ओ, वा, वी, वो — रोहिणि
   ಒ, ವಾ, ವೀ, ವೋ — ರೋಹಿಣಿ
   O, Va, Vee, Vo — Rohini

5. वे, वो, का, के — मृगशिरा
   ವೇ, ವೋ, ಕಾ, ಕೇ — ಮೃಗಶಿರ
   Vay, Vo, Kaa, Ke — Mrigasira

6. कू, घा, ङ, छ — आरिद्रा
   ಕೂ, ಘಾ, ಜ್ಞ, ಛ — ಆರಿದ್ರಾ
   Koo, Ghaa, Jna, Cha — Aridra

7. के, को, हा, ही — पुनर्वसु
   ಕೆ, ಕೋ, ಹಾ, ಹೀ — ಪುನರ್ವಸು
   Kay, Ko, Haa, Hee — Punarvasu

8. हू, हे, हो, डा — पुष्यमि
   ಹೂ, ಹೇ, ಹೋ, ಡಾ — ಪುಷ್ಯಮಿ
   Hoo, Hay, Ho, Daa — Pushyami

Appendix

9.	डी,	डू,	डे,	डो	— आश्लेषा
	ಡೀ,	ಡೂ,	ಡೇ,	ಡೋ	— ಆಶ್ಲೇಷಾ
	Dee,	Doo,	Day	Do	— Aslesha
10.	मा,	मी,	मू,	मे	— मख
	ಮಾ,	ಮೀ,	ಮೂ,	ಮೇ	— ಮಖಾ
	Maa,	Mee,	Moo,	May	— Makha
11.	मो,	टा,	टी,	टू	— पूर्वफलगुनी
	ಮೋ,	ಟಾ,	ಟೀ,	ಟೂ	— ಪೂರ್ವಫಲ್ಗುಣಿ (ಪುಬ್ಬ).
	Mo,	Taa,	Tee,	Too	— Pubba
12.	टे,	टो,	पा,	पी	— उत्तरा
	ಟೇ,	ಟೋ,	ಪಾ,	ಪೀ,	— ಉತ್ತರಾ
	Tay,	To,	Paa,	Pee	— Uttara
13.	पु,	षा,	णा,	ठा	— हस्ता
	ಪು,	ಷಾ,	ಣಾ,	ಠಾ	— ಹಸ್ತಾ
	Pu,	Shaa,	Naa,	Thaa	— Hasta
14.	पे,	पो,	रा,	री	— चित्ता
	ಪೇ,	ಪೋ,	ರಾ,	ರೀ,	— ಚಿತ್ತಾ
	Pay,	Po,	Raa,	Ree	— Chitta
15.	रु,	रे,	रा,	ता	— स्वाती
	ರು,	ರೇ,	ರಾ,	ತಾ	— ಸ್ವಾತಿ
	Ru,	Ray,	Raa,	Tha	— Swati
16.	ती,	तू,	ते,	तो	— विशाखा
	ತೀ,	ತೂ,	ತೇ,	ತೋ	— ವಿಶಾಖಾ
	Thee,	Thoo,	Thay,	Tho	— Visakha
17.	ना,	नी,	नू,	ने	— अनुराधा
	ನಾ,	ನೀ,	ನೂ,	ನೇ	— ಅನುರಾಧ
	Naa,	Nee,	Noo,	Nay	— Anuradha
18.	नो,	या,	यी,	यू	— ज्येष्ठा
	ನೋ,	ಯಾ,	ಯೀ,	ಯೂ	— ಜ್ಯೇಷ್ಠಾ
	No,	Yaa,	Yee,	Yoo	— Jyeshta

19.	ये,	यो,	बा,	बी	—	मूला
	ಯೇ,	ಯೋ,	ಬಾ,	ಬೀ	—	ಮೂಲಾ
	Yay,	Yo,	Baa,	Bee	—	Moola
20	बु,	धा,	भ,	ढा	—	पूर्वाषाढा
	ಬು,	ಧಾ,	ಭ,	ಢಾ	—	ಪೂರ್ವಾಷಾಢಾ
	Bu,	Dhaa,	Bha,	Dha	—	Poorvashadha
21.	बे,	बो,	जा,	जी	—	उत्तराषाढा
	ಬೇ,	ಬೋ,	ಜಾ,	ಜೀ	—	ಉತ್ತರಾಷಾಢಾ
	Bay,	Bo,	Jaa,	Jee	—	Uttarashadha
22.	जु,	जे,	जो,	घ	—	श्रवण
	ಜು,	ಜೇ,	ಜೋ,	ಘ	—	ಶ್ರವಣ
	Ju,	Jay,	Jo,	Gha	—	Sravana
23.	गा,	गी,	गू,	गे	—	धनिष्ठा
	ಗಾ,	ಗೀ,	ಗೂ,	ಗೇ	—	ಧನಿಷ್ಠಾ
	Gaa,	Gee,	Goo,	Gay	—	Dhanishta
24.	गो,	सा,	सी,	सू	—	शतभिष
	ಗೋ,	ಸಾ,	ಸೀ,	ಸೂ	—	ಶತಭಿಷ
	Go,	Saa,	See,	Soo	—	Satabhisha
25.	से,	सो,	दा,	दी	—	पूर्वाभाद्र
	ಸೇ,	ಸೋ,	ದಾ,	ದೀ	—	ಪೂರ್ವಾಭಾದ್ರ
	Say,	So,	Daa	Dee	—	Poorvabhadra
26.	दु,	थ,	ज्ञ		—	उत्तराभाद्र
	ದು,	ಥ,	ಜ್ಞ,		—	ಉತ್ತರಾಭಾದ್ರ
	Du,	Tha,	Jna		—	Uttarabhadra
27.	दे,	दो,	चा,	ची	—	रेवति
	ದೇ,	ದೋ,	ಚಾ,	ಚೀ	—	ರೇವತಿ
	De,	Do,	Chaa,	Chee	—	Revati

The nakshatra of a person is known from the first letter of the name. Take for instance, the name Varaha or Vance. The first letter is Va. In the above table Va falls in the 4th line, 2nd row, suggesting that the constellation is Rohini 2. Take James. It falls in line 22,

Appendix

2nd row. The constellation is Sravana 2 and the Janma Rasi would be Makara. In case of conjoint words, the first letter alone has to be taken. Thus for Krishna, the first letter should be taken as Ka and hence the nakshatra would be Mrigasira 3 (5th line, 3rd row).

Panaparas.—The 2nd, 5th, 8th and 11th.

Planetary Aspects.—All planets aspect the 7th house powerfully. Sani, Guru and Kuja have special aspects or Visesha Drishti, viz., the 3rd and 10th, 5th and 9th, and 4th and 8th respectively.

Planets.—Ravi or the Sun, Chandra or the Moon, Kuja or Mars, Budha or Mercury, Guru or Jupiter, Sukra or Venus, Sani or Saturn, Rahu or Dragon's Head and Ketu or Dragon's Tail.

Planets and the Human Body.—

Mesha	Head
Vrishabha	Face
Mithuna	Neck
Kataka	Chest
Simha	Stomach
Kanya	Waist
Thula	Sexual Organ
Vrischika	Belly
Dhanus	Thighs
Makara	Knees
Kumbha	Buttocks
Meena	Feet

Planets, Combustion of—Planets situated within distances mentioned below from the Sun become combust :—

The Moon within		12°
Mars	"	17°

Mercury	''	14°*
Jupiter	''	11°
Venus	''	10°*
Saturn	''	15°

Planets, Female.—The Moon and Venus.

Planetary Hours. - This is based on the arrangement of the solar system as it exists in nature. According to *Surya Siddhanta*, Saturn is the most distant planet from the Earth. Next come in regular order, Jupiter, Mars, Sun, Venus, Mercury, the Moon and the Earth. The first hour of the day is governed by the lord of the day. The other hours follow according to the order given above. Thus on a Sunday, lord of the 1st hora is the Sun ; that of the 2nd is Venus ; 3rd Mercury ; 4th Moon ; 5th Saturn ; 6th Jupiter ; 7th Mars ; 8th Sun ; and finally the 24th Mercury. The lord of the 25th hour (the 1st hour on Monday) is evidently the Moon. The table given on page 159 will be found to be useful to students of astrology.

Planets, Male.—The Sun, Mars and Jupiter.

Planets, Neutral.- Mercury, Saturn.

Radical.—Pertaining to the birth.

Rahukalam.—When the sunrise is 6 a.m., Rahukalam will rule at the following times :—

Sunday	—	4-30 p.m. to 6-00 p.m.
Monday	—	7-30 a.m. to 9-00 a.m.
Tuesday	—	3-00 p.m. to 4-30 p.m.
Wednesday	—	12-00 noon to 1-30 p.m.
Thursday	—	1-30 p.m. to 3-00 p.m.
Friday	—	10-30 a.m. to 12-00 noon
Saturday	—	9-00 a.m. to 10-30 a.m.

Shodasa Karmas.—Sixteen kinds of pre-natal and post-natal ceremonies which the Hindu is enjoined to undergo.

---

*When Mercury and Venus are retrograde, the orb will be one degree less.

Appendix

	Sunday	Monday	Tuesday	Wednesday	Thursday	Friday	Saturday
1	Ravi	Chandra	Kuja	Budha	Guru	Sukra	Sani
2	Sukra	Sani	Ravi	Chandra	Kuja	Budha	Guru
3	Budha	Guru	Sukra	Sani	Ravi	Chandra	Kuja
4	Chandra	Kuja	Budha	Guru	Sukra	Sani	Ravi
5	Sani	Ravi	Chandra	Kuja	Budha	Guru	Sukra
6	Guru	Sukra	Sani	Ravi	Chandra	Kuja	Budha
7	Kuja	Budha	Guru	Sukra	Sani	Ravi	Chandra
8	Ravi	Chandra	Kuja	Budha	Guru	Sukra	Sani
9	Sukra	Sani	Ravi	Chandra	Kuja	Budha	Guru
10	Budha	Guru	Sukra	Sani	Ravi	Chandra	Kuja
11	Chandra	Kuja	Budha	Guru	Sukra	Sani	Ravi
12	Sani	Ravi	Chandra	Kuja	Budha	Guru	Sukra
13	Guru	Sukra	Sani	Ravi	Chandra	Kuja	Budha
14	Kuja	Budha	Guru	Sukra	Sani	Ravi	Chanpra
15	Ravi	Chandra	Kuja	Budha	Guru	Sukra	Sani
16	Sukra	Sani	Ravi	Chandra	Kuja	Budha	Guru
17	Budha	Guru	Sukra	Sani	Ravi	Chandra	Kuja
18	Chandra	Kuja	Budha	Guru	Sukra	Sani	Ravi
19	Sani	Ravi	Chandra	Kuja	Budha	Guru	Sukra
20	Guru	Sukra	Sani	Ravi	Chandra	Kuja	Budha
21	Kuja	Budha	Chandra	Sukra	Sani	Ravi	Chandra
22	Ravi	Chandra	Kuja	Budha	Guru	Sukra	Sani
23	Sukra	Sani	Ravi	Chandra	Kuja	Budha	Guru
24	Budha	Guru	Sukra	Sani	Ravi	Chandra	Kuja

Signs.—Mesha or Aries, Vrishabha or Taurus, Mithuna or Gemini, Karkataka or Cancer, Simha or Leo, Kanya or Virgo, Thula or Libra, Vrischika or Scorpio, Dhanus or Sagittarius, Makara or Capricorn, Kumbha or Aquarius and Meena or Pisces.

Signs, Airy.—Gemini, Libra and Aquarius.

Signs, Blind.—Aries, Taurus, Leo are day-blind; Gemini, Cancer and Virgo are night-blind.

Signs, Common.—Gemini, Virgo, Sagittarius and Pisces.

Signs, Deaf.—Libra and Scorpio cannot hear in the morning. Sagittarius and Capricorn become deaf in the evening. Cancer and Virgo are deaf at midday.

Signs, Earthy.—Taurus, Virgo and Capricorn.

Signs, Fiery.—Aries, Leo and Sagittarius.

Signs, Fixed.—Taurus, Leo, Scorpio and Aquarius.

Signs, Lame.—During twilight Aquarius and Pisces become lame.

Signs, Movable.—Aries, Cancer, Libra and Capricorn.

Signs, Watery.—Cancer, Scorpio and Pisces.

Tithis, Different kinds of.—Nanda—the 1st, 6th and 11th lunar days are known as *Nanda*. *Bhadra.*—the 2nd, 7th and 12th lunar days. *Jaya.*—the 3rd, 8th and 13th lunar days. *Riktha.*—the 4th, 9th and 14th lunar days. *Poorna.*—the 5th, 10th and 15th lunar days.

Thridoshas.—According to Ayurveda, health is maintained by a certain equilibrium of three fundamental humours or doshas, viz., Vatha (wind), Pitha (bile) and Sleshma (phlegm).

Trikonas.—The 1st, 5th and 9th.

Upachaya.—The 3rd, 6th, 10th and 11th signs from Lagna.

Vainasika.—This denotes the 22nd constellation from that of one's birth. It indicates destruction and should be avoided for all good work.

Yogas, Bad.—Of the 27 yogas mentioned in Appendix III the following are inauspicious :—Vyaghatha, Parigha, Vajra, Vyathipatha, Vydhriti, Ganda, Atiganda, Soola, Vishkambha.

APPENDIX II

(Table of Nakshatras)

Sl. No.	Nakshatra	Longitude from beginning of Aries ° '
1.	Aswini	— 13 20
2.	Bharani	— 26 40
3.	Krittika	— 40 00
4.	Rohini	— 53 20
5.	Mrigasira	— 66 40
6.	Aridra	— 80 00
7.	Punarvasu	— 93 20
8.	Pushyami	— 106 40
9.	Aslesha	— 120 00
10.	Makha	— 133 20
11.	Pubba	— 146 40
12.	Uttara	— 160 00
13.	Hasta	— 173 20
14.	Chitta	— 186 40
15.	Swati	— 200 00
16.	Visakha	— 213 20
17.	Anuradha	— 226 40
18.	Jyeshta	— 240 00
19.	Moola	— 253 20
20.	Poorvashadha	— 266 40
21.	Uttarashadha	— 280 00
22.	Sravana	— 293 20
23.	Dhanishta	— 306 40
24.	Satabhisha	— 320 00
25.	Poorvabhadra	— 333 20
26.	Uttarabhadra	— 346 40
27.	Revati	— 360 00

APPENDIX III

(Table of Yogas)

Sl. No.	Yogas	Longitude from beginning of Aries
		° '
1.	Vishkambha	— 13 20
2.	Priti	— 26 40
3.	Ayushman	— 40 00
4.	Saubhagya	— 53 20
5.	Sobhana	— 66 40
6.	Atiganda	— 80 00
7.	Sukarman	— 93 20
8.	Dhriti	— 106 40
9.	Soola	— 120 00
10.	Ganda	— 133 20
11.	Vriddhi	— 146 40
12.	Dhruva	— 160 00
13.	Vyaghata	— 173 20
14.	Harshana	— 186 40
15.	Vajra	— 200 00
16.	Siddhi	— 213 20
17.	Vyatipata	— 226 40
18.	Variyan	— 240 00
19.	Parigha	— 253 20
20.	Siva	— 266 40
21.	Siddha	— 280 00
22.	Sadhya	— 293 20
23.	Subha	— 306 40
24.	Sukla	— 320 00
25.	Brahma	— 333 20
26.	Indra	— 346 40
27.	Vaidhriti	360 00

EXPLANATION

Suppose the sum of the longitudes of the Sun and the moon is $281°$. Reference to the above table reveals Siddha Yoga lasting from $280°$ to $293° 20'$. Therefore one degree has elapsed in this yoga.

BIBLIOGRAPHY

Muhurtha Chinthamani
Muhurtha Marthanda
Muhurtha Darpana
Muhurtha Deepika
Kalamrita
Uttara Kalamrita
Prasna Marga
Brihat Samhita
Kala Prakasika
Jatakadesa Marga
Muhurtha Pradarsini
Vidya Madhaveeyam
A Text-Book of Astrology—By Dr. A. J. Pearce
Astrological Mirror (Big Edn.)
　　　　　　　　—By Prof. B. Suryanarain Rao
Astrological Mirror (Pocket Edn.)
　　　　　　　　—By Prof. B. Suryanarain Rao
An Introduction to Astrology—By Prof. B. Suryanarain Rao
Electional Astrology — By V. E. Robson
Actions of Radiations on Living Cells— By D. E. Lea
The Secret of Life—By Georges Lakhovsky
Astrology and Modern Thought—By Dr. B. V. Raman
Hindu Predictive Astrology—By. Dr. B. V. Raman

INDEX

A

Abhijit 23
Accountants 98
Acidity 37
Actors 98
Aditi 23, 28
Adhobhaga Nalayaha 90
Adverse Yogas 25
Agni 23, 26
Agnipanchaka 19, 20
Agreeability 55
Agriculture see Crops 35
Ahi 28
Ahibudhya 23
Ahirbudhya 28
Air 108
Ajaikapat 23
Ajipada 28
Akalagharjitha Vrishti 30
Aksharabhyasa 49 see also
  Auspicious Ceremonies
Akshi 90
Alcibiades 57
Alkalinity 37
Alphabet (Aksharabhyasa)
  21, 49

America 54
Amita Siddha Yoga 33
Amnion 43
Anabolism 39
Andreas Sparre 41
Animal 99 see Buying
Annaprasana 48 see also
  Auspicious Ceremonies
Anodes 39
Ant-hills 99
Anujanma 45
Anuradha 23
Apamarga 36
Apple 145
Aquarius 13
Aquatic sign 115
Aryama 28
Ardhama 86
Aridra 23
Aries 13
Arms buying 138 see also
  Buying
Artha 54
Artists 98
Aryaman 23
Ascites, treatment for 131
Ashadha 84, 103

Ashtakavarga of Venus in marriage 59
Ashtama Lagna 29
Ashtami 147
Aslesha 19, 23, 26, 82
Aspasia 57
Astrologer 143
Astrology 1
Aswi 28
Aswini 14, 23
Athens 57
Atiganda 26
Atmosphere 105
Attraction 105
Auspicious Ceremonies and Works 23, 24, 25 see also Tarabala, Chandrabala, Panchaka, Mahadoshas, Siddha Yogas
Authors 98
Autumn 116
Ayana 136
Ayurvedic 114
Ayushman App. III

B

Bacteria 114
Balava 13
Banian 44
Bankers 98
Barley 118 see Crops
Baptising 14 see also Namakarana
Bavakarana 12

Beans 117
Beards 91
Beets, sowing 116
Bernard Macfadden on Sex 37
Betelnuts 117 see Crops
Bhadra Karana 26
Bhadrapada 103
Bhaga 23, 28
Bharani 14, 24, 26, 147
Bhasmas 114
Bhootas 108
Bhootabali 109
Bhrigu 80
Bhrigu Shatka 29, 143
Bhujanga 13
Billiousness 129
Bindus 59
Biogenetic 37
Birds 120 see Buying
Biology 2
Birth star 16
Blindness 52
Bluhm, Prof.—His experiments 37
Booksellers 98
Borrowing 92 see Money
Botany 114
Brahma 90
Brahman 23
Brahmadanda 89
Brahmins 50
Brain 44
Brass 91 see also Buying

Index

Bride 29 see also Kutas
Bridegroom 29 see also Kutas
Brihaspathi 80
Brihat Samhita 23, 136
Buddhisthana 90
Buffalo 70 see Cattle
Bugbear 82
Building cities and towns 134 see also Auspicious Works
Buildings 103, 110
Business 92 see also Buying and Mahadoshas
Butchers 98
Buying 21, 91, 92 see also Tarabala, Chandrabala and Panchaka
Buying Houses 111
Buying Lands for Houses 20, 104 see also Auspicious Works 21, 109
Buying Land for Agriculture 116
Buying Cows, Horses, Sheep, Dogs 128

C

Cabbage 117 see Crops
Calamus viminalis 107
Camille Flammarion 115
Cancer 13, 29
Capricorn 13
Carl Jung 6
Carpenters 98
Carrots, sowing 117 see Crops
Cat 70
Cathodes 39
Cato's dictum 115
Cattle, collecting fodder 24 see also Buying and Karana
Cauliflower 118 see Crops
Cell 39
Century 105
Cereals 118 see Crops
Chaitra 51, 85
Chance 43
Chandrabala 18, 143
Chandra Garbha 125
Chandrashtama 31
Charaka on change of sex 41, 44
Chara constellation 130
Charm 99
Chatushpada 13
Chemistry 37
Chemists 98
Chitta 14, 23
Chora panchakam 20
Chowlam 48 see also Auspicious Ceremonies
Chromosomes 37
Cicero 57
Civil servants 98
Climacteric 14
Climatic 54

Clothes 86 see also Tarabala and Chandrabala
Cocoanuts 118 see Crops
Co-habitation 35
Cohesion 101
Coitus 36
Combust—Jupiter and Venus in 46, 48
Commanders 98
Common Janma Nakshatra 80
Common Janma Rasis 80
Compatibility 54
Competitions, success in 137 see also Auspicious Works
Compositors 98
Conception and development of the embryo 40, 43, 144
Connubial dissatisfaction 132
Constellations—fixed, light, sharp, soft, movable dreadful and mixed 23, 24
Constellations and their lord or presiding Devatas 23
Consummation 35
Consumption, treatment for 130
Contigencies 79
Copper 90 see also Buying

Copulation 36
Coronation 21, 23, 135 see also State
Cosmic determinism 1
Cosmic force 100
Cosmic radiation 6
Councillor 98
Cow 70, 120 see also Buying and Selling
Cradling 48 see also Auspicious Ceremonies
Creepers 118 see Crops
Critical period 15
Crops 116 see Sowing and also Reaping
Crops, in-gathering 119
Crops, harvesting 119
Cucumbers 115, 117 see Crops

D

Dairy Farms 135 see also Building
Dancing 23, 97
Danger 104
Darwin 39
Davenport, findings of 37
Daughter, birth of an eldest 36, 146
Deafness 91
Death 59 see Kutas
Deceit for 24

Index 169

Deeds evil, violent and cruel 26
Deflorations 34
Delusion 88
Democratic Government, formation of 135
Demetrius 57
Dental treatment 131
Dentition 14
Designer 102
Destruction 29
Determinism 141
Destructive constellations 81
Deva Gana 68
Dhanishta 14, 23
Dhanus 116
Dhanya Parvatha Yoga 120
Dharma 54
Dharma Sastras 95
Dickens 57
Digestion 90
Digging wells 106
Dina Kutam 67
Diseases, treatment 148 see also Treatment
Disharmony 68
Dismantling Buildings 111
Divining, water 107
Divorce 68
Diurnal Muhurtha 28
Doctor 100
Dog 70, 120 see also Buying

Door frame, fixing 105
Doshas 24, 82, 83 see also Mahadoshas
Dosha Swalpa 25
Dual personality 41
Durmuhurtha 27
Dysgenic 54

E

Ear Boring 48 see Karna Vedha
Eclipses 30
Economic subject 95
Education, commencing see Aksharabhyasa and Chapter XI
Ego development in marrying partners 77
Ekargala 30
Ekavimsati Mahadoshas 25
Electional 1
Elections, Miscellaneous 137
Electricity 4, 10
Electromagnetic 22, 113
Elephant 70
Embryo 42
Emergent occasions 25
Empirical 1
Enemas, taking 131
Energy-principle, conservation of 90
Engineering 103
Enteric 130

Entry into New House 103, 107 see also Auspicious Works
Environments 114
Epilepsy, treatment 130
Ethnological 54
Etymology 40
European 40
Evils 31
Evolution 69, 114
Example on Kutas 67, 68, 72, 74, 75
Exceptions 69, 75

F

Factory Workers 98
Fertilisation 39
Fever 129, 130
Ficus indica 44
Fig 115
Fine Arts 23
Fire-proof 105
Fire, setting 24
First-feeding 14, 21, 48
Fixed signs 13 see Appendix
Fixing the Door Frame 103, 105 see also Auspicious Works
Fodder 24
Foetus 36, 43
Flower plants 118 see also Planting
Fools 88
Forces 4
Fortification 32
Foundation 23, 103, 105 see also Laying
Friday 26, 33
Fruition 31
Fuel collecting 24

G

Gana Kutam 68, 145
Ganda 26
Gandanthara 29
Garbhadhana 35
Gardening 23
Garga 51, 80
Garija 13
Garlic 117 see Crops
Gebhard, Prof. 4
Gemini 13
General Matters, Elections concerning 88, 93, 147
Genitals 44
Germs 11
Gestation 43
Ghati 13
Gingelli, sowing 117 see also Crops
Girisa 28
Glands 41
Gonorrhoea, treatment 130
Gotra 54
Grains, sowing see Crops
Grafting plants 115, 119
Graha Maitri 69, 73, 145
Grahanothpatha 30

Greeshma 115
Grete 42
Gridhra 13
Griha Pravesam 110
Guna Bahulya 25
Guru 52

H

Hair 89
Halos 136
Happiness 73, 104 see also Kutas
Hard-rock while digging wells 107
Hare 70
Harvesting see Crops
Hasta 14
Hastam 90
Hawkers 98
Heal 112
Heart 43
Heat 113
Herbs 115
Heredity 54
Hesiod 115
Hindus 50, 77, 86
Honey-comb 99
Hora 96 see Appendix
Horoscopy 3, 140
Horse 70, 120 see also Races, Buying and Selling
Horse radish 115

House-building, repairing, etc., 20, 23, 98, 103 see also Panchaka and Mahadoshas
Hostile pairs 71
Hridi 97
Humours 78
Husband and wife separation, discord, attachment, subservience, unhappiness, etc, 57, 59 see also Kutas

I

Ignorance 81
Ill-matched 57
Immoral 97
Imprisonment 23
Incantations 23
Incendiarism 104
India 54
Indra 23
Indragni 23
Industries, starting of 23
Infidelity, marital 55, 87
Infra-red 114
Inherent 18
Inheritance 38
Inhibitions 7
Inimical Yonis 71
Initiations 26
Injections, taking 131
Insurance Agents 98

Intellect 51, 98
International problems 148 see also Public
Interdependence 113
Investiture of Sacred Thread see Upanayana
Investment 112
Invoking spirit 23
Iron 91 see also Buying

J

Janaki 48
Janma Nakshatra 16, 20
Janma Rasi 16
Janma Tara 7, 21
Jaya 33
Jaya Yoga 86
Jeeva 28
Jeevaka 45
Jewellers 98
Jewellery 92 see also Buying
Jewellery see Travel
Judge 98
Junctions 79
Jupiter 3
Jyeshta 14, 23, 26, 82, 146

K

Kalaprakasika 136
Kalapurusha 1
Kalka 45
Kalamrita 136
Kama 54

Kantharajju 76
Karana 8, 12, 26
Karma 3
Karna Vedha 48 see also Auspicious Ceremonies
Karthari Dosha 27
Kartika 85
Katabolism 39
Katirajju 76
Kaulava 13
Kendra 32 see Appendix
Kerala Sastra 83
Ketu 52
Kill 113
Kimstughna 13
Kings 97
Krishna 47
Kitchner, Lord 123
Krittika 14, 24, 26, 147
Kshatriya 77
Kshipram constellation 86 see Appendix
Kúja 58
Kuja Dosha 83
Kujashtama 29, 143
Kukshi 90
Kunavamsa 57
Kutas 54, 67, 75 see also Contingencies, Destructive csnstellations, Kuja Dosha, Summary

L

Lagna, its fortification 33
Lagna Thyajya 13, 31

Index

Law suits, filing 136 see also Auspicious Works
Lawyers 98
Laying the foundation 23, 103, 105 see also Auspicious Works
Learning 21, 97 see also education
Leeks 115
Legatee 94
Lending 92 see Money
Lettuce 117
Leo 13, 29
Leprosy, treatment 130
Libra 13
Library, forming a 143 see also Mahadoshas
Life 2
Life Force 39
Life-saving
Lifeless 114
Light 4
Lilies 115
Lion 70
Litigation 92
Little-heads 102
Loha 114
Longevity 49 see also Kutas
Lotteries see Competitions
Luck 102
Lunar month 9
Lunar movements 89

M

Magha 51
Magistrates 98
Magnetism 4
Mahadoshas 25, 143
Mahapatha 30
Maharshis 2
Maharshi Yoga 86
Mahendra 69
Mahendra Yoga 86
Makha 14, 24
Making a Will 94
Maladjustments 55, 87
Mammals 69
Manes 23
Mantras getting and other initiations 27
Manusha Gana 68, 69
Margasira 85
Marriage 14, 17, 87, 144 147 see also Tarabala, Siddha Yogas, Chandrabala, Panchaka, Mahadoshas, Seasons in Andhra, Karnataka and Tamilnadu 84 Electing a time 84-85
Mars 48
Mary Powell 57
Masha 44
Mathematicians 98
Mathematics 2
Maxillary processes 43

Mechanics 98
Medhra 90
Medical Elections 128
Medicine, administration of 19, 21, 23, 102 Preparation 132
Meditation 27
Melons 118 see Crops
Membranes 43
Men 35
Menopause 15
Menses 40
Menstruation 39
Mental currents 26
Mercury 3
Mesha 18
Metals 114
Metaphysics 10
Midwives 98
Military Quarters, building 135 see also Building
Mill-hands 98
Milton 57
Mimamsa 95
Mineral 103
Ministers 98
Misery 73
Mitra 16, 23, 28
Moksha 54
Monday 36
Money 92, 93 see also Tarabala, Chandrabala and Panchaka
Mongoose 70
Monkey 70
Moola 14, 23, 81
Moon 5, 10
Mother 82
Movable signs 13 see Appendix
Mrigasira 14, 23
Mrityu Panchaka 20
Muhurtha 10, 28, 141, 142
Muhurtha Thathwa 80
Murders 23
Music 23, 95
Mythology 108

N

Nabhi 90
Nabhirajju 76
Nadi Kuta 67, 77, 78
Naga 13
Naidhana Tara 16
Nail cutting 91
Nakshatra 8, 10, 26 see also Constellations
Nakshatra Panchaka 24
Naktanchara 28
Namakarana 26, 47 see also Auspicious Ceremonies
Nama Tara 7, 146 see also Appendix
Nanda 34
Narada 80
National problems 149 see also Public
Natural Forces 95

Index

Nature 68
Navami 147
Navamsa Lagna 27
Nefarious, Schemes for 24
Negative period 14
Nicolai K. on Sex 38
Niruti 23
Nisheka 35, 144 see also Nuptials
Nocturnal Muhurta 28
Nonsense 102
Nose treatment 132
Nuptials 18, 21, 35 see also Tarabala, Chandrabala, Panchaka, Mahadoshas
Nurses 98

O

Obalachari 42
Obalamma 42
Occupation 20
Olive 114
Omen 101
Onion 115, 118 see Crops
Operations, Surgical 131
Organism 37
Ornamentation 23
Ovum 39
Ovary 39

P

Padarajju 76
Paddy 118 see Crops
Padas 78
Palalo 5
Palmyra seedlings 118 see also Crops
Panacea, preparation 132
Panchaka 18, 20, 142
Panchanga 8, 142
Panchanga Suddhi 26
Papa Shadvarga 29
Parents 146
Paramamitra 16
Paris 41
Parturition 42
Parvathi 47
Pathological 38
Peace, making 139 see also Auspicious Works
Pearls 98
Peach 117 see Crops
Pea trees 118
Pepper 118 see Crops
Perfumers 98
Periodicity
Permanency 101
Permanent Karanas 13
Pericles 57
Phalguna 50
Phaseolus radiatus 51
Phases of Moon and diseases 128
Physics 2
Physiological 14, 78
Pilgrimage 25, 147 see also Travel

Pisces 13, 29
Pishta
Pitha Nakshatra 78 see Constellations
Pitru 23, 28
Planetary friendships 74, 75
Planetary rays 2
Planting trees 2, 23 117, 118
Pleasures 23
Plasm 43
Plato 56
Pledging 93
Ploughing the land 116
Plutarch 115
Plum 117 see Crops
Poisoning 24
Political Department 98
Political Sciences 95
Pollution 91
Post-natal ceremonies 14, 47
Potatoes, sowing 117 see Crops
Poverty see Kutas
Pratyak Nakshatra 16, 20
Prajapathi 25
Prasna Marga 58
Preceptors 98
Precious metals 98
Pregnancy 35
Prejudices 87
Pre-natal ceremonies 14, 35 see also Nisheka
Printers 98

Prisoners, seeking escaped 138
Prosperity see Kutas
Priya Yoga 86
Processes 2
Procession, going on 23
Progeny 35 see also Kutas
Pseudo-sexologists 54
Psycho-astrological 53
Psychological 14 78
Pubba 14, 24
Puberty 14
Public Matters 133 see also Auspicious Works
Puja 105
Pumpkins 118 see Crops
Pumsavana 35, 36, 45 see also Tarabala, Chandrabala, Panchaka and Mahadoshas
Punarvasu 14, 23
Purchaser 110
Purgative taking 131
Purna 34
Purushnta 28
Purusha 107
Puruththam see Kutas
Poorvabhadra 14, 24
Poorvashadha 14, 24
Pushan 23
Pushya 14, 23, 24, 143
Pushya Yoga 86

Q

Quadrants 46

Index

R

Races, Horse. 137 see also Buying
Radiation 2
Radishes 115, 118 see Crops
Ragi, sowing 117 see Crops
Rahu 13, 52
Raja Panchakam 19
Raja Yoga 106
Rajju Kuta 67, 75
Rakshasa Gana 68, 69, 145
Rama 47
Ramakrishna 89
Rasi Kuta 67, 73
Rasyadhipathi 67, 73
Rat 70
Reaping the Crop 119
Recovering money due 93
Religious rites 27
Removing to another house 112 see also Shifting
Repairing 24
Reproduction 35
Residential 112
Resonance 6
Revati 14, 24, 26
Rheumatism, treatment for 129
Rhythms 39
Rice 117 see Crops
Riktha 34 see Appendix
Rishabhaka 45
Rishis 24, 89
Rogapanchakam 20
Rohini 14, 23
Root crops 118 see Crops
Rudhitam 52
Rudra 23, 28
Rundhram 52
Rye 118 see Crops

S

Sacerdotal fire 82
Sacred Thread 50
Sacrifices 20
Sadhana 16
Sadharana constellations 131 see Appendix
Saffron 115
Sagittarius 13, 29
Sagraha Chandra 27
Sahachara 45
Sakuna or Sakini Karana 13, 26
Samdram 28
Sampat 16
Samudra 86
Sankha 46
Sanskrit 43
Santhis 114
Sarcastical heckling 108
Saraswati Yoga 85
Sastras 54
Satabhisha 14, 23
Sathamukhi 28
Saturday 13, 34, 143
Saturn 51

Savita 23
Scavengers 98
Scheming—nefarious 23
Scientists 37
Scholar 98
School Master 98
Scorpio 13, 29
Sea Voyages 127 see also Journey
Secretaries 98
Secretion 42
Seemantha 46 see also Tarabala, Chandrabala Panchaka and Mahadoshas
Selling 93, 120 see also Panchaka, Sense gratification
Separation of friends, etc., 23, 58
Serpent 23
Servants, Employing 88 see also Panchaka
Sesamum 118 see Crops
Sex, changing of 37, 144
Sexology 36
Sexual union 21, 23, 35
Sex-urge 70
Shares 88
Shashtashta Vipagatha Chandra Dosha 27
Shaving 21, 88, 90
Sheep 70, 93, 120 see also Buying and Selling
Shifting from place to place 93 see also Mahadoshas
Ship-building and launching 134 see also Auspicious Works
Ship-wrecks, social 58
Shodasa Karmas 14, 144
Short-sightedness 108
Siddha Yoga 33
Sidereal activity 2
Sight 91
Sira 90
Sirorajju 76
Site 99
Sky 108
Sleshma Nakshatra 77
Socrates 56
Soil 107
Solonum indicum 118 see Crops
Soldiers 98
Solicitors 98
Son, birth of an eldest 36, 146
Soola 26
Sound 49, 113
South, Journey towards 24
Sowing 23, 115, 117, 118
Special Yogas 33
Special Considerations 79
Spectrum analysis 114
Spermatozoa 89
Spirits 23
Spoorjitham 52

Index

Sport 23
Spuritham 52
Square 58
Sravana 16, 23, 135
Sreenatha Yoga 86
State, electing Head of the 135
Stead, Mr. 123
Steel 91 see also Buying
Stellar influences 101
Sterility 38
Stree-Deergha 67, 69
Stree-purva 80
Strongholds, destroying 139
Stigma 20
Strength of constellation 16
Subordination 98
Sudra 77
Sugarcane 118 see Crops
Summer crops 115
Summary 141, 151
Sun 2
Sunday 34
Sunlight 113
Superstition 108
Superstructure 105 see Building
Surveyors 98
Suryanarain Rao, B., 2, 151
Surya Sankramana 26
Swashta 23
Swati 14

T

Taithula Karana 12, 26
Tamilian, Marriage
Tarabala 16, 20
Taurus 13
Temperament see Kutas
Temples, building 135
Terentia 57
Testator 94
Theeshna 93
Theft 89, 109
Thieves 103
Thithi 9, 142 see Appendix
Tithi Gandanthara 29
Thomas Carlyle 57
Thrijanma 36
Thula 116
Thursday 26, 33
Thury, Prof.—his theory 37
Thyajyakala 14
Thyasthur 28
Tides 39
Tiger 70
Timber 115
Titanica, destroyed 123
Time 1, 2, 121
Tomato planting 117 see Crops
Tom fooleries 102
Tonsure see Chowlam
Tools 91 see also Buying
Trade 92

Travel 20, 21, 23, 121, 127
see also Tarabala,
Chandrabala and
Panchaka
Travel : Short, long 127
pilgrimage—Air Business,
by water see Treatment,
beginning 126, 127
Trees, felling 150
Trines 46
Tropic of Cancer 49
Tuesday 13, 26, 31, 143
Turnips 115
Typhoid 130

U

Udararajju 76
Udayastha Suddhi 27
Ugra constellations 48, 130
Ugra Yogas 130
Ultra-violet 114
Under-currents 107
Units of agreement for
marriage 67
Unterberger, Prof. on sex 37
Upachayas 110 see
Appendix
Upanayanam 20, 21, 50, 52,
144 see also Auspicious
Ceremonies
Upatsu 90
Utensils 91 see also Buying
Uttara 14, 23
Uttarabhadra 14, 23

Uttarashadha 14, 23
Uttarayana 108

V

Vahni 19
Vaisakha 51, 85
Vaisya ego 77
Vaksha 90
Vara 8, 26, 28
Varahamihira 105
Varna 67, 77
Varuna 23, 28
Vasishta 55
Vasya Kuta 67, 75
Vasu 23, 28
Vastu Purusha 103
Vastu Sastra 99, 147
Vatha Nakshatra 77
Vatsyayana 90
Vayu 23
Vedangas 95
Vedas 95
Vedha 67, 76
Vegetable 113
Vehicles, acquiring of 23
Venereal diseases,
treatment 130
Venus 31
Vessels 91
Vetasa 107
Vibration 2, 22
Vidhatru 28
Vidhi 28

Index

Vidya 95, 98 see also Aksharabhyasa
Vidya Yoga 96
Vijaya Yoga 86
Vines 111
Vipat Nakshatra 16, 17
Virgo 13
Visakha 14, 24, 82
Visha Ghatika 29
Vishnu 23, 28
Vision 50
Visvedeva 23, 28
Vitality 8
Visti 13
Vrishabha 81
Vyatipata 26, 30
Vydhruti 26, 30, 31

W

Wandering couple 76
War 21 Starting, 139 see also Auspicious Works
Warriors 98
Waste 90
Watery planet 107
Watery signs 107 see Appendix
Wearing new apparel 23 see also Cloth
Wedlock 53
Wednesday 31
Weekday, How to remove the blemish 31
Wheat 118 see Planting
Whitewashing 111
Widowhood 56
Wife 38
Wills see also Auspicious Works
Wine-sellers 105
Woman's Janma Nakshatra 21
Womb of time 4
Worship 103

X

Xantippe 56

Y

Yama 23, 28
Yatra 147 see Travel
Yatraphani Chakra 125
Yoga 12, 142
Yogas adverse and their neutralisation 25, 30 see Appendix
Yogini 125
Yoni Kuta, Male and Female, etc., 69, 70, 71
Yumigadyuti 28

Z

Zeno 57

Vayu 95, 98 see also
Aksha abhyasa
Vidya Yoga 96
Vitarya Yoga 96
Vijnas 111
Vibet Nakshatra 16, 17
Vinoa 3
Visakha 14, 24, 92
Visas Charitra 29
Vishon 23, 29
Vision 64
Visvedeva 23, 26
Vitality 6
Vishi 12
Vrishabha 61
Vyupida 26, 30
Vyatirini 28, 30, 31

W
Wandering sonarios
War 21 Stations, 138 see
also Auspicious Works
Warriors 58
Waste 60
Willow planet 107
Water, signs 107 see
Achara X
Wearing new apparel 23
see also Cloth
Weapons 83
Wedeeshs 23

Weekday, How to remove
the blemish 31
Wheat 13 see Planting
Whitewashing 112
Widowhood 86
Wife 38
Wife see also Auspicious
Works
Wine-sellers 106
Women's teams
Nakshatra 27
Womb at time 4
Worship 103

X
Xanjiype 66

Y
Yama 22, 28
Yatra 147 see Travel
Yerraplani, Chakra 125
Yoga 12, 142
Yoga advises and their
Remanahas 26, 98 see
Apedika
Yogini 128
Yoni Kota, Male and
Female etc. 65, 70, 71
Yunupdavati 29

Z
Zodi 27